Crochet
for Absolute *Beginners*

3 BOOKS IN 1

2024 Edition

Crochet
for Absolute Beginners

Learn How to Crochet. A Complete Step-by-Step Guide with Easy Instructions and Colored Illustrations.

3 BOOKS IN 1

2024 Edition

VD Publishing

Printed in United States of America
10 9 8 7 6 5 4

To all those who enjoy doing things with their own hands.

CONTENTS

Crocheting is a simple, enjoyable, and accessible craft. It's a fantastic pastime to have because it takes very little equipment and can be carried everywhere with you. To get started, all you need is a ball of yarn in your favorite color, a hook and a pair of scissors, and with a little patience, you'll be making designs in no time. You'll learn all the fundamental knots and patterns in this book so you can start crocheting your own simple yet lovely items.

Before tackling the more intricate knots, it will be beneficial if you master the very fundamental knots. All knots and patterns will be based on the fundamental slip knot, which you will learn how to perform in this book. It will also provide you with a few designs to follow in order to produce basic yet lovely items.

Learning to crochet will be a great project to embark on. To begin your new activity, go to your local craft store and select a hook that is most comfortable for your hands. Then you may select from a variety of vibrantly colored crochet yarns. Crochet is a great and simple method to express you. Allow your imagination to go wild. Your crocheted items may not be as flawless as you'd like them to be at first, but with experience, you'll be able to create stunning necklaces, bracelets, and bags. You may even make your own outfit with crochet.

Crochet is a relaxing and enjoyable pastime that anybody may participate in. It can help you stay productive even when things aren't going well. You may do this while standing in line, driving, or taking the bus. It may even aid in the reduction of stress. You may relax and de-stress by doing repeated actions. The finished product is a lovely handcrafted item that you can keep and appreciate, or perhaps give as a present.

Chapter 1

Prepare Your Materials

You'll need some basic equipment before getting started. Crochet hooks, shears, a row counter, stitch markers, and a tote or bag to keep your yarn and unfinished projects, and tools are all included. You don't have to spend a lot of money to have decent equipment. All you really require to get started is a quality set of metal crochet hooks, a good pair of scissors, and some basic stitch markers. We'll go through the fundamental equipment you'll need and how to utilize it in this chapter.

Crochet Hooks

Hook Anatomy

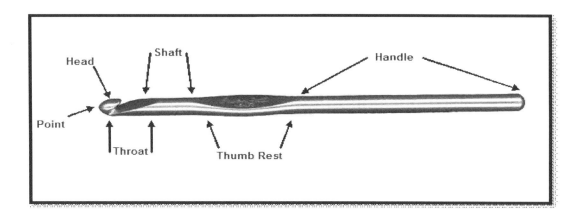

The tip, head, shank, throat, thumb rest, and handle are the basic components of a crochet hook. A pointier tip makes it easier to get into tight stitches, but a rounder tip is less likely to tear the yarn. The yarn is caught in the neck, and the stitch size is determined by the shank, which retains your working loops. The head form varies depending on the manufacturer. Tapered hooks have a more curved form and a smaller neck than in-line hooks, which have the head in line with and the same size as the shank.

The thumb rest makes it easier to operate and swivel the hook, and the handle keeps it balanced when crocheting. If you have large hands, a longer grip could be more comfortable. If you have trouble grasping a crochet hook, look for one with a cushioned or curved handle.

Crochet hooks range in size from tiny, needle-like hooks used with thread to gigantic hooks used to make carpets. It is recommended getting a nice quality hook set with sizes ranging from US E to US K for the beginners. These will be the standard sizes for most patterns, regardless of ability level. If you have arthritis or difficulty grasping a hook, you can find hooks with comfortable grips. You may also use clay to construct your own grips. Steel, bamboo, different woods, and plastic are some of the other materials utilized for hooks. A set of high-quality metal hooks is ideal for beginners and will last for many years.

A crochet hook is a straightforward prey item. The grip or pad on most hooks is an indentation in the handle that you use to grab the hook. Lips and thread guides are divided into two categories. Boye hooks feature a rounded thread guide, whereas Bates hooks have an angular thread guide. It's entirely up to you the sort of hook you use.

Tunisian crochet is something you might wish to try as your skills improve. A long hook is used to hold the stitches in this form of crochet. It resembles a long knitting needle with a crochet hook attached to one end. Tunisian crochet hooks with a lengthy piece of plastic or metal to hold several stitches are also available. These needles have a hook on one end and resemble circular knitting needles. For really big projects, such as Afghans, circular Tunisian crochet hooks are utilized. Double-ended crochet hooks are also available. These can be used for more advanced Tunisian crochet techniques.

Crochet Hook Sizes

Crochet hooks are available in a variety of sizes. Steel hooks with really small hook sizes are utilized for fragile thread and lace work. Steel hooks are not the same size as other hooks. When utilizing steel hooks, keep in mind that the larger the number, the smaller the hook; for example, the greatest hook size is 00, and the lowest is 14.

Crochet hook sizes range from US E/4 (3.5mm) to US K/10.5 in most patterns (6.5mm). Both the leer and millimeter sizes are used by patterns. To refer to the various hook sizes, use this helpful chart.

This chart is also useful if you come across patterns that aren't written in US language.

Hook Size (Metric)	US Equivalent Size	UK Equivalent Size	Hook Size (Metric)	US Equivalent Size	UK Equivalent Size
0.60mm	16		4.00mm	G/6	8
0.75mm	14		4.50mm	7	7
1.00mm	11	4	5.00mm	H/8	6
1.25mm	10	3	5.50mm	I/9	5
1.50mm	8	2.5	6.00mm	J/10	4
1.75mm	6	2	6.50mm	K/10.5	3
2.00mm	-	14	7.00mm	-	2
2.25mm	B/1	-	8.00mm	L/11	0
2.50mm	-	12	9.00mm	M/N/13	00
2.75mm	C/2	-	10.00mm	N/P/15	000
3.00mm	-	11	12.00mm	O/16	-
3.25mm	D/3	10	15.00mm	P/Q/19	-
3.50mm	E/4	9	19.00mm	S/35	-
3.75mm	F/5	-	20.00mm	-	-

Hook Materials

Crochet hooks are generally constructed of metal or plastic, but wood or bamboo hooks are also available. Although aluminum is smooth, sturdy, and long-lasting metal can feel chilly and rigid in the hands. Wood is warm and flexible, but it must be thoroughly finished to avoid rough places that catch yarn and conditioned to prevent it from drying out. Plastic is smooth and affordable, but when used with some yarns, it creates a squeaky noise and bends or breaks quickly. Bamboo is light and flexible, yet it can splinter or shatter, especially in smaller quantities.

Each material has advantages and disadvantages, so sample a few to discover which you prefer before purchasing numerous sizes.

How to Hold a Crochet Hook?

When it comes to crochet hook handling, there are two schools of thought.

The pencil grip is one, while the knife grip is another. If you utilize a pencil grip, your hook will be held like a pencil, as the name implies. You'll be holding your hook like a table knife if you utilize a knife grip. Both methods are valid, and they result in the same stitches. It's entirely up to you which hold you'll employ. Try both and see which one you like.

Pencil position

Grip the hook like a pencil to keep it in this place. Place the contoured thumb rest over your thumb and beneath your index finger if the hook has one. If the hook does have a thumb rest, the middle of your thumb should be about 2 inches (5cm) from the point of the hook, and you should also grip a hook without a thumb rest here.

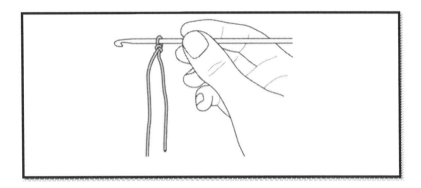

Knife position

To grip a crochet hook in this manner, grasp it as if you were cutting food with a table knife. If the hook includes a thumb rest, place your thumb and index finger in this contoured part, with the middle of your thumb approximately 2in (5cm) from the hook point. Grip a hook with your thumb resting at the same level as the tip.

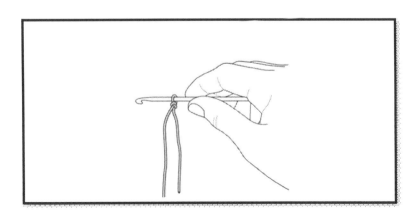

Choosing Your Yarn

Crochet offers a vast selection of yarns to work with, which is one of the numerous advantages of the craft. However, with so many options, it may be daunting at times.

So, which yarn should you choose, particularly if you're a beginner crocheter? When you're just getting started, a smooth yarn that feels wonderful in your hands is the ideal option. Choose a basic, soft yarn in a color you like, but at first, stay away from excessively dark hues. With lighter-colored yarn, your stitches will be more visible. Currently, novelty yarns like loops, fluff, bobbles, or glitter are appealing, but they're more difficult to work with. Wait until you have a firm handle on the fundamentals of crochet before attempting to work with one of these yarns since the texture obscures your stitches.

Whatever yarn you pick, it will most likely arrive in a ball, skein, or hank, surrounded by a paper ball band. The yarn's weight, fiber composition, yardage, care recommendations, and other details are all included on the ball band.

Animal Fibers

Animal fibers such as mohair, angora, wool, alpaca, and silk are used to make yarn. Wool is a popular choice since it produces a fabric with a lot of warmth and stretch. Wool is made from sheep and comes in a variety of colors and weights.

Alpaca yarn is made from the same-named mammal and has a shine to it. It's also really warm and pleasant to the touch. Alpaca yarn is a good substitute for wool, and the cloth has a wonderful drape.

Mohair yarn is made from the fibers of goats. Young goats produce mohair yarn, but older goats produce coarser mohair. Mohair yarn may be dyed in a variety of vibrant colors and retains them well.

The hair from the underbelly of a certain breed of goat is used to make cashmere yarn. The Angora rabbit is the source of Angora yarn. Both types of yarn are really luxuriant. Both types of yarn have a lovely drape to them. These yarns are fairly pricey, but they're a joy to work with.

Silk fibers are derived from silkworms and are usually combined with other fibers to provide yarn strength, sheen, and texture. Silk is a popular addition to yarn, and there are some stunning examples available.

Plant Fibers

Yarn created from plant fibers is extremely durable and colorfast. Plant fiber yarns are a little fiddly to work with at first, but they're great for kitchen and bath goods, as well as summer clothes.

Cotton fibers are utilized to make a strong and durable material. It is available in a variety of weights, ranging from delicate coon thread for doilies and lace work to bulky weight yarn for mats and carpets.

Bamboo is also used to generate a highly strong yarn with a shine that is superior to cotton. Bamboo-thread-crocheted fabric provides a lovely stitch definition and a beautiful drape.

Linen yarn is made from flax fibers. Linen is a great fabric for summer clothes since it absorbs away moisture and breathes well. It's long-lasting and available in a variety of colors.

Another strong plant-based yarn is made from hemp fibers. Any item that asks for coon or bamboo may be made with hemp yarn. It's available in a range of colors and textures.

Synthetic Fibers

Acrylic yarn is one of the most common forms of yarn. Acrylic yarn is made from petroleum-based synthetic fibers. It may be colored in a variety of colors, is long-lasting, and simple to deal with. Acrylic yarn comes in a variety of thicknesses, from fine fingerling yarn to thick chunky bulky yarn. Acrylic yarn is available in a variety of textures. It's simple to work with and has a little give, making it ideal for beginners.

Acrylic yarn with beads, sequins, and other decorations is available. Acrylic eyelash yarn is a lot of pleasure to work with. It includes little strands that mimic eyelashes and is used in conjunction with other yarns to make incredibly detailed decorations on a variety of projects. Another fun acrylic yarn is fun fur. With this sort of synthetic yarn, you may simply make faux fur accessories.

Polyester, Nylon, and microfiber are examples of synthetic yarn. To give flexibility, shine, and texture, these fibers are usually combined with other types of yarn.

Weights of Yarn

Yarn is available in a variety of weights, ranging from fingerling for lace work and baby goods to extremely thick. Yarn weight is measured using a standardized technique used by yarn producers.

STANDARD YARN WEIGHT SYSTEM
Categories of yarn, gauge ranges, and recommended hook sizes

Yarn Weight Symbol & Category Names	1 SUPER FINE	2 FINE	3 LIGHT	4 MEDIUM	5 BULKY	6 SUPER BULKY
Type of Yarns in Category	Sock, Fingering, Baby	Sport, Baby	DK, Light Worsted	Worsted, Afghan, Aran	Chunky, Craft, Rug	Super Chunky, Roving
Crochet Gauge* Ranges in Single Crochet to 4 inch	21–32 sts	16–20 sts	12–17 sts	11–14 sts	8–11 sts	5–9 sts
Recommended Hook in Metric Size Range	2.25–3.25mm	3.5–4.5mm	4.5–5.5mm	5.5–6.5mm	6.5–9mm	9mm and larger
Recommended Hook– U.S. Size Range	B1–E4	E4–7	7–I9	I9–K-10½	K-10½–M-13	M13 and larger

Information about the Yarn Label

All of the information you require to choose the right yarn for your project may be found on the yarn label. The fiber composition, dye lot number, weight, care, gauge, and suggested hook size are all listed on a yarn label. For a newbie, comprehending the information on a yarn label is essential. You'll go through the information on yarn labels in this topic so you may make the best decision possible when shopping for yarn.

A set of standardized yarn care symbols is used by the majority of major yarn producers. Although private label and artisan yarns may not use these symbols, most major companies, such as Lion Brand, Red Heart, Paton and Caron do.

The gauge is one of the most significant pieces of information on a yarn label. Gauge refers to the number of stitches per row and the number of rows required making a four-by-four-inch swatch. The gauge is mentioned in almost every design. Before beginning a design, crochet a four-by-four-inch square using the required hook size and compare the number of stitches per row and the number of rows you finish up with to the pattern's stated gauge. If your gauge is greater, you'll need to tighten the tension or use a smaller hook. If your gauge is smaller than the pattern, ease your tension or use a bigger hook.

When you're first starting out, don't forget to make a gauge swatch. It will save you time and money, so develop the habit to use them.

Skeins, Balls, and Hanks

The majority of yarn sold in stores is packaged in skeins. Skeins are simple to use and don't require the yarn to be rolled into balls. To keep the yarn from tangling, make sure you pull it from the center.

If the yarn is packaged in a ball, you can use it without rerolling it. To protect the yarn ball from rolling away while you're working with it, place it in a tiny bowl.

Hanks are available in a variety of animal fiber and hand spun yarns. Don't even attempt to work from a hank. You'll have a knotted mess on your hands. Rolling Hanks into balls or cakes is required. There are electric and manual yarn winders available, both of which will save you time and hassles. Swifts are often used with winders to keep the yarn in place while it is wrapped. Expand the swift to accommodate the hank of yarn, thread the winder, and wind the yarn into a ball or cake gently.

How Much Yarn Will You Require?

You need to understand how much yarn to buy when crocheting following a pattern. Each design specifies how much length (yardage) of each weight of yarn is needed to finish the item, so choose a yarn of similar weight and check the yardage on the ball band. Divide the yardage provided in the pattern by the yardage from one ball and round up to the nearest whole number to get how many balls of yarn you'll need.

Yarn is colored in batches, with subtle color variations between each batch. Check each ball band to confirm that each ball comes from same numbered dye lot to guarantee that all of the yarn you buy is the same hue.

The Tools You Need

Crochet's portability is one of its appeals. You simply need a ball of yarn, a hook, and sometimes a pattern to get started. A few extra tools, on the other hand, can make things easier.

Scissors

Crochet scissors are a must-have item. You'll need them to cut the yarn at the end of each section and to finish your work by trimming the yarn tails. To create clean, precise cuts, use a tiny, sharp pair.

Yarn Needle

To weave in your yarn tails and sew pieces together, you'll need a yarn needle (also known as a darning needle or tapestry needle). Yarn needles are broad, blunt-tipped needles with a large eye to accommodate the yarn. Metal needles are superior to plastic needles, which flex and shatter readily.

Measuring tape

When it comes to verifying your gauge (tension) and the size of your final items, a measuring tape (or ruler) is indispensable. A retractable measuring tape is a useful tool to have in your crochet kit because it's tiny and portable, and you never know when you'll need it.

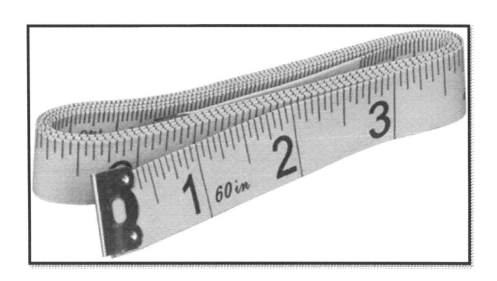

Stitch markers

Stitch markers can be used in a variety of ways. You may use stitch markers to identify certain stitches in your crochet so you don't forget your position in the pattern, and you can also place a stitch marker in the working loop to keep your work from unravelling when you set it down.

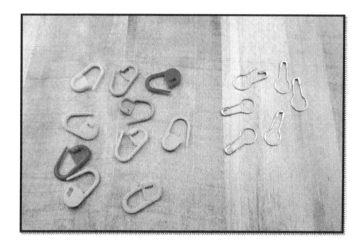

Pins

If you're going to block your crochet, you'll need pins. T-pins are an excellent option. They're long, strong, and simple to work with. Make careful to use rustproof pins to avoid rust stains damaging your work.

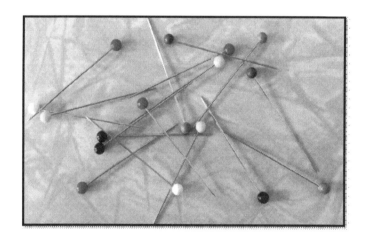

Other Useful Tools

If you're working on a large piece or are easily sidetracked, a row counter will come in handy. You'll never lose your position if you remember to increment the counter at the end of each row.

All of your crochet equipment is kept together in a case. There's no need for anything extravagant. A pencil box or compact cosmetic bag should hold all of your needs. When you've amassed a collection of hooks, keep them in a pen cup on your desk or organize them by size in a roll-up cloth bag with a pocket for each hook.

Chapter 2

Get Started with Crochet

Making a Slipknot

To begin crocheting, tie a slipknot between your yarn and your hook.

• Make a circle with your fingers

Drape the yarn over one or two fingers and wrap it around them to make a loop, leaving a 6-inch (15-cm) tail hanging down over your left hand.

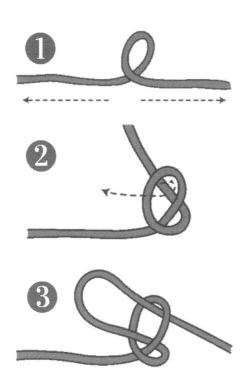

- Place your hook here

Remove your fingers from the loop and hold it between your fingertip and a thumb while inserting your hook into it.

- The working yarn should be caught

With your hook, catch the working yarn. (Not the small beginning tail, but the working yarn that goes to the yarn ball.)

- Make it work

Pull the yarn up through to the loop with the hook.

- Pull the knot tighter

To tighten the knot, pull on the yarn ends.

- The working yarn should be pulled

To close the loop around your hook, pull the working yarn.

- Allow it to hang free

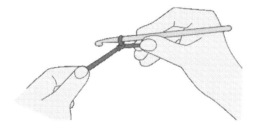

Allow enough room within the loop for your hook to smoothly move up and down.

You've made an adjustable slipknot if you ever need to pull on the starting tail rather than the working yarn to stiffen the slipknot around the hook (a knot that can loosen itself). To begin crocheting, you'll need a secure knot, so if you've formed an adjustable slipknot by accident, undo it and start over.

Making a Yarn Over

One of the most important crochet techniques is the yarn over (YO). Although it may appear that you wrap the yarn all around hook with your left hand, it is really faster and simpler to keep your left hand steady and grab the yarn with your hook:

- Take the yarn and turn it over

Pass your hook beneath the yarn, allowing the yarn to hang over the hook. The working yarn (which goes to your left hand) is on the hook's left side. Make sure the working yarn will be on the right side of the hook by not passing the hook over it and catching it from above. This causes your sutures to twist.

- And once more

Swing the hook over and down under the yarn in the same manner to yarn over twice.

- Make three loops in total

On your hook, you now have three loops: the working loop, the yarn wrapped twice around the hook, and the yarn wrapped two times around the hook.

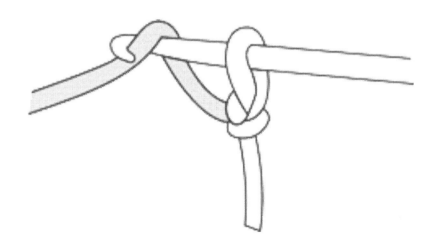

Making a Foundation Chain

The foundation chain runs all along bottom of your crocheted creation and serves as a basis for your stitches to be worked into.

- Make a slipknot with your yarn

Begin by tying a slipknot on your hook.

- Yarn over

Bring it over.

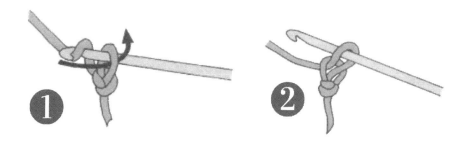

Pull your hook back through to the loop you've already created.

- And that's it

You have one chain currently (abbreviated ch)

After you yarn over, rotate the hook toward you to make it simpler to draw the yarn through your stitches. It's less likely to snag on your sutures if the hook's head is pointing sideways.

- Keep going

For each subsequent chain, repeat steps 1 and 2. Hold on to the stitches you've previously chained with your left hand to assist support the chain as you draw your hook through. Every few stitches move your hand up the chain to keep the chain near to your hook.

Making your chains seem consistent will take some practice. Despite the fact that a sloppy chain may appear messy, resist the impulse to neaten your chain stitches by pushing on the yarn to shrink the stitch. The stitch becomes a knot as a result of this action. That's not what you're looking for. A crocheted chain should be flexible and open so that you can easily put your hook back into each chain loop.

Chain Counting

When you look at your chain from the front, the side that faces you while you crochet, it should resemble a row of Vs. Each of these Vs is made up of a single chain stitch. Start counting your chains from the V above the slipknot and work your way up to your hook. The functional loop on your hook is what you're looking for. This isn't a stitch, so don't count it.

Label every 10 or 20 chains using a stitch marker to make counting simpler when building a lengthy foundation chain. If you're unsure, especially if you're working with a large beginning chain, add a few more chains to make sure you've got enough. If you have too many extras after completing the first row, you may easily unravel them. If you don't have enough chains, you'll have to unwind the entire first row to add them.

Basic Crochet Techniques

We'll go through the basic crochet methods you'll need to know as a beginner in this topic. Crocheting in the round, changing colors at the beginning and middle of a row, joining yarn when you run out or it breaks, and other crochet methods will be covered.

Crocheting in the Round

This technique may be applied to a variety of projects, including hats. Insert the hook into the first chain after you've formed your foundation chain, yarn over, and drag the yarn between the chain and the loop on the hook. This is referred to as joining. Attaching a stitch marker to the connecting chain is strongly recommended. You now have a stitched circle. It will be difficult to identify where the round begins once you begin going around your project.

You'll see that your seam is shifting diagonally as you crochet in the round. This is typical, and it's just how the patterns develop. This is especially true if your weight has fluctuated during the pattern. While counting your stitches has always been crucial, it is especially critical while crocheting in the round to ensure that your item turns out correctly.

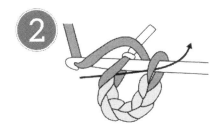

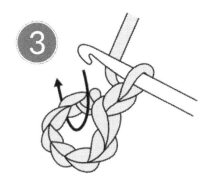

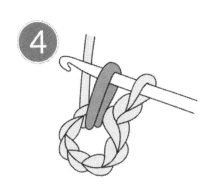

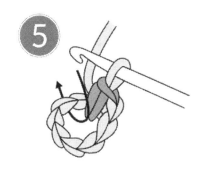

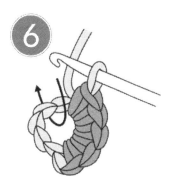

Magic Ring

This technique may be applied to a variety of projects, including hats. Insert the hook into the first chain after you've formed your foundation chain, yarn over, and drag the yarn between the chain and the loop on the hook. This is referred to as joining. Attaching a stitch marker to the connecting chain is strongly recommended. You now have a stitched circle. It will be difficult to identify where the round begins once you begin going around your project.

You'll see that your seam is shifting diagonally as you crochet in the round. This is typical, and it's just how the patterns develop. This is especially true if your weight has fluctuated during the pattern. While counting your stitches has always been crucial, it is especially critical while crocheting in the round to ensure that your item turns out correctly.

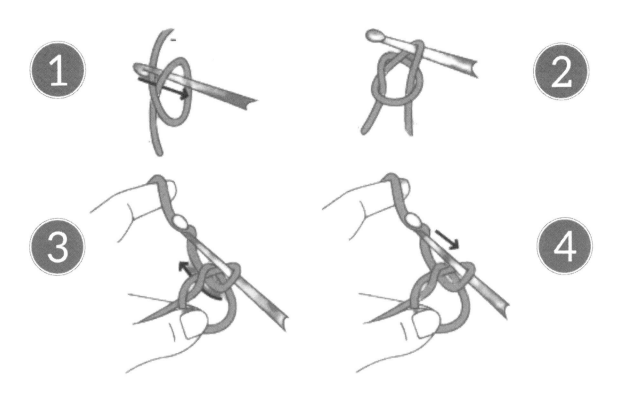

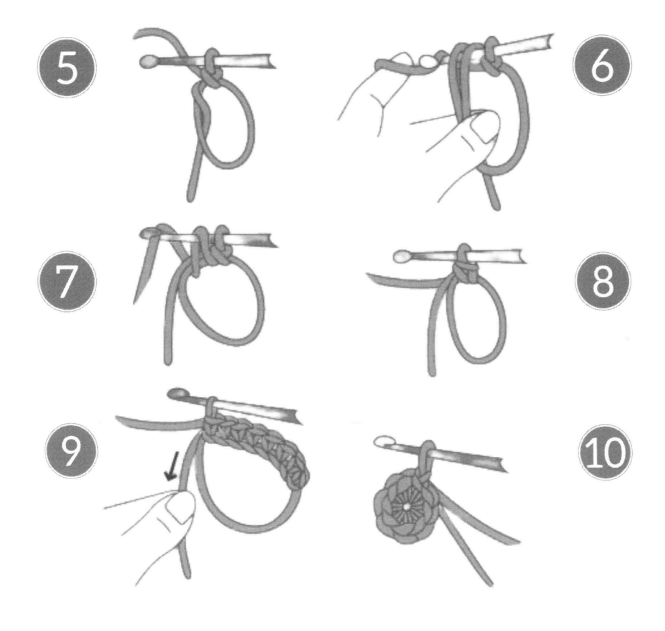

Changing Colors

One of the most enjoyable aspects about crochet is experimenting with different colors. Changing colors may appear to be a difficult undertaking for a newbie, but it is actually rather simple. If you wish to change colors after finishing a row, simply work the last knot unless you have two loops on the hook. Draw the new color across the two loops using your new color. Turn your work over and chain threads for the first stitch of the following row, carefully pulling the old and new colors together. Leave a six-inch tail of the previous color to weave in.

You may use the same method to change colors in the middle of a row. Grab the new color and draw it through the last stitch of the previous color until you have two loops on the hook. Work a few more stitches before pulling the colors together. If you pull them too tight, your cloth will pucker. To weave in later, leave a six-inch tail.

There are a few strategies you can employ to keep those pesky tails under control so you don't have to weave them in at the end. The yarn tails can be caught under the new stitches. To do so, make sure your hook gets under the tails of both the new and old colors and captures them in your stitches until the tails are gone. Another option is to weave the tails in and out of the previous row's stitches before crocheting; making sure the hook is below the tails. This is a great technique to keep your tails tight and prevent having to weave in a lot of them later.

Joining Yarn

- **Spit Splicing**

Only animal fiber yarns, such as alpaca, cashmere, wool, and other forms of animal fibers, may be used using the first approach. Plant and synthetic yarns do not naturally feel up, so do not attempt to utilize this approach on them. Yes, spit will be used. Your spit includes enzymes that aid in the breakdown of yarn fibers, and when combined with the heat generated by pressing your palms together, the yarn felts and connects itself organically.

Fray the ends of both the old and new yarns first. Now lick your hands' palms and arrange the yarns in one hand, overlapping the ends. Rub your palms together firmly until all of the strands are combined into a single strand. It's possible that you'll have to massage the splice a few times to get it to hold. You may continue crocheting now that you have one continuous strand of yarn.

- **Russian Join**

Any sort of yarn fiber can be utilized with the Russian join method. This method of yarn joining necessitates the use of a tapestry needle. Sew the yarn back on itself for a few inches by threading the needle with one of the strands of yarn. Thread the needle with the other strand of yarn. Sew the second piece of yarn back on itself by bringing the needle up through the loop made by sewing the first yarn back on itself. Pull the ends of both strands together in opposing hands until they meet in the center. Once the yarn is linked, you may need to cut the frayed ends.

Both of these techniques produce extremely strong connections that are nearly unnoticeable in your crocheted fabric. If you're working with a thick yarn, you might notice a little more weight where the yarn is linked, but it won't distract from the end product.

Chapter 3

How to Read Crochet Patterns?

C rochet terminologies and fundamental crochet stitches are the first steps in learning the basics of crocheting.

Understanding the Symbols Of Stitching

Crochet symbols are hand-drawn crochet stitches that are frequently shown in a pattern diagram for crocheting and create a pattern when performed in the correct order. It is critical that you comprehend all of the symbols used in the pattern you select.

Each crochet sign creates a unique crochet stitch when combined with other symbols. As a result, do not skip a single stitch; otherwise, you may not achieve the required design.

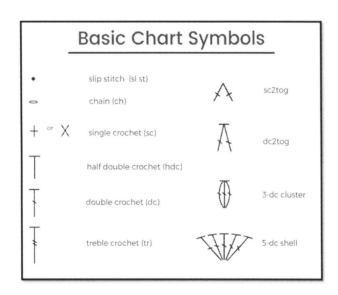

Difficulty

Each crochet pattern is assigned a level of difficulty. It denotes the pattern's level of intricacy. There are numerous difficulty levels to choose from:

- Beginner
- Easy
- Intermediate and higher levels
- Experience

This isn't to say that if you chose a complicated pattern, you won't be able to duplicate it. Even a beginner may create patterns of unlimited complexity by following the tutorials.

However, experts still propose that you study patterns in stages, beginning with the basic level and progressing to the advanced level.

Tools and Materials

A list of necessary materials and tools is included in the second note on the pattern page. This normally includes information like as yarn kind, scissors, hook size, stitch marker, tapestry needle, and so on.

Crocheting materials have distinct properties, thus in addition to the brand; other criteria such as weight, length, and size are shown in the diagram for the yarn. This is done so that you may find the correct yarn from another producer and receive a similar product.

The hook size is determined by the yarn being used. You'll need to pick the hook size if you're using a different yarn in terms of characteristics and composition. The suggested hook labels are usually indicated on each yarn brand's label.

Crocheting tools are extras that may make the process easier and more fun. To make a pom-pom, for example, a specific gadget exists that allows you to make an even, gorgeous pom-pom in a matter of minutes.

Gauge

A gauge pattern is a little crocheted pattern that is used to determine the size of a project. It's used to see if you've selected the appropriate crochet and yarn. Gauge corresponds to how many rows and stitches must be knitted to achieve the desired size in crochet patterns.

Crochet a little section of the design and check the sizes stated in the diagram: if they're bigger, use a smaller hook; if they're smaller, use a bigger hook.

You may also rinse and iron the sample if you choose. This will give an indication of how the final product will react to it and what you should focus on.

Abbreviations

Crochet abbreviations are usually found at the start of a design or in the or the front or back of a crochet pattern book. Because acronyms might vary across designs, it's usually better to refer to the precise abbreviations provided for the pattern you're working on if they're available. However, if you come across a design that is lacking its abbreviations, this list of popular crochet phrases and their abbreviations might be useful in determining what to do.

Most Common Crochet Terminology and Abbreviations

For the convenience, here is a list of the most frequent crochet terminology and their acronyms, organized alphabetically:

- **Beg:** Begin stands for start, as in the beginning of a row.
- **BL**: stands for "back loop" crochet and may alternatively be spelled BLO ("back loop only"). When used in this way, BL can also indicate to blocks or bobbles peculiar to the design. Always check the design's stitch list for this information, which is normally located at the beginning of every pattern.

- **BP** stands for "back post," which means you're stitching around the post rather than through the loops, and especially around the back post. This is usually used in conjunction with the stitch's abbreviation. Back post single crochet, for example, is bpsc, whereas back post double crochet is bpdc. For a related crochet term/abbreviation, see "FP" below.

- **Ch (s)**: stands for chain (s). Since virtually all crochet designs begin with chains, this is one of the most common acronyms you'll see. Many of them also feature chains in their designs. This is one of the crochet terminologies you'll rapidly recall as a newbie crocheter learning the language of the craft.

- **Cl**: stands for cluster. Cluster stitches come in a variety of styles; your design should explain the one you'll use. 3 tr cluster, for example, is a cluster of three treble crochet stitches. However, "cl" stands for clusters in general.

- **Dc**: stands for double crochet, and is one of the most frequent crochet stitches.

- **Dec**: stands for reduction, and it's a crochet shaping method.

- **Dtr**: Double treble crochet is abbreviated as dtr. This is one of the taller fundamental crochet stitches, only a hair higher than treble crochet.

- **FL**: In contrast to BL/ BLO, FL stands for "front loop," often shortened FLO or "front loop alone."

- **FO**: stands for completed object. This phrase is not always used in crochet designs, but it is a popular acronym among crafters when discussing their work on the internet.

- **FP**: stands for front post, as opposed to the previously mentioned "back post."

- **Hdc**: Half double crochet (hdc) is a fundamental crochet stitch that is halfway between single and double crochet in height.

- **Inc**: Increase is a similar approach to reducing (dec) that is used in shaping.

- **Incl**: including / include / inclusive.

- **Oz**: stands for ounce/ounces, which may be found on yarn labels or in the section of crochet designs that tells you how much yarn you'll need. Other units of measurement include grammes (g), metres (m), and yards (yd).

- **PM**: stands for "place marker."

- **Pc:** stands for popcorn, a textured crochet stitch that looks like clusters or bobbles. Patterns that use these stitches generally provide instructions on how to make the stitch at the beginning of the pattern, along with the designer's chosen crochet abbreviation.

- **Rep**: repeat; this is usually used in conjunction with symbols indicating the pattern component to be repeated. * = The pattern specifies how many times a set of instructions should be repeated after an asterisk or between asterisks.

- **()**: The pattern will describe how many times a set of instructions supplied inside parentheses should be repeated.

- **[]**: The pattern will indicate how many times a series of instructions given inside the brackets should be repeated.

- **Rev**: stands for reverse and is sometimes used in conjunction with other acronyms such as rev sc, which stands for reverse single crochet stitch.

- **Rnd(s)**: round(s), a counting term used while working in circles or in other circular situations (in contrast to working in rows).

- **RS**: When crocheting in rows, there is a "right side" and a "wrong side," and either one might be facing, thus it can be beneficial to identify them as some designs do.

- **Sc**: Single crochet is one of the most common and fundamental crochet stitches.

- **SK**: skip; for example, the phrase SK ch indicates that you may omit the next chain and proceed into the next one (ship chain).

- **sl st**: slip stitch, which is both a means for joining rounds in crochet and a stitch in and of itself.

Sp (s): space(s).

St (s): stitch (es).

Tog: together; this is frequently substituted for dec (rease) in phrases like "sc2tog" to signify a decline in single crochet stitch.

Tr: stands for triple crochet/ treble crochet, which is another typical crochet stitch.

Tr Tr: triple treble crochet, a taller crochet stitch than the dtr mentioned above.

UFO (unfinished object) is a crochet term that is more commonly used in written communication between crocheters than in designs.

WIP: stands for "work in progress," and it's similar to a UFO, only the WIP is usually in advancement while the UFO has been laid aside and isn't being worked on.

WS: stands for wrong side, which is the polar opposite of right side (rs).

YO: stands for yarn over, and it's a step in practically every crochet stitch. It's not commonly found in crochet designs, but it's regularly seen in crochet stitch explanations.

Measurements/Sizing

The sizes of the final goods are indicated on each diagram. When it comes to clothing, for example, you may select a variety of sizes. This was made so that you may crochet a garment with the pattern you choose without having to figure out and model everything yourself.

As a rule, such measurements are denoted by / or brackets (). So, in order to avoid becoming confused and crochet exactly the clothing you want, we propose printing out the crocheting description and marking the sizes with a marker. As a result, if you follow their instructions, you will never make an error when crocheting.

What Kinds Of Stitches Are Used?

Each crochet design has its own set of stitches. Make sure you're familiar with all of the terms before you start crocheting. Check out our introductory lessons if one of them appears odd to you and you're having trouble completing it.

You can go on to the following step once you've learned and practiced all of the stitches required for crocheting.

What methods and techniques are employed?

All patterns are classified into several categories based on the processes used to create them, each with its own set of characteristics. Only double crochet and chain stitches are utilized in the fillet method, for example.

Instructions for Making the Pattern

The textual pattern instruction, which explains you the step-by-step work method, is the largest and most comprehensive section. Depending on the pattern, the crocheted item may be separated into multiple sub-pieces that must be brought together at the end. These can be individual motifs, resulting in plaid, or openwork patterns, resulting in an attractive outfit. In any event, you'll need to learn all of the stages of work thoroughly before you begin crocheting. In addition, you'll discover all of the abbreviations and phrases that weren't decoded at the start of the written pattern below. If you forget or are unsure about an abbreviation, go back to the beginning of the pattern page.

Row vs. Round

Crochet designs are either crocheted in rows or in rounds. Depending on the design, you'll be working in rounds, rows, or a combination of both. The following are the primary distinctions between crocheting in rows and crocheting in rounds: Round crochet is when you crochet in a circle and end each row with a slip stitch. Row crochet involves crocheting in a straight line and turning the work over at the end of each row.

The key to completing a design successfully is determining the crocheting progress correctly.

Getting The Pattern Started

You'll need to start with a slip knot whether you're crocheting in the round or in rows. Because it thinks you already know, the pattern doesn't always tell you this. The only time this isn't true is when you're making a magical circle.

The following instructions will show you how to tie a slip knot —

The pattern repeat – a fundamental element that denotes a component of the pattern that may be repeated many times when growing the project – is occasionally included in the instruction for the convenience of users.

Every crocheted creation, on average, starts with a series of chain stitches known as the Foundation chain.

For instance, consider the following foundation chain: multiples of 8+1.

Or

17 links in the foundation chain

In the first scenario, multiples refer to an 8-loop pattern, or the number of times the pattern may be repeated. This is done so that you may adjust the design to the size you choose. To crochet several repetitions, or repeats, add 8 the needed number of times: 8 + 8 + 8 +... then add one loop at the end.

In the second scenario, it is stated that a chain of 17 loops is required to complete the pattern.

Create a slip knot on your hook (remember, the instructions never say to do this), then make multiples of 8+1 or 17 chain stitches, loosely. Count these chains carefully, and don't include the slip knot in your count. A stitch is never counted while the loop on the hook is present.

You now have a foundation chain and need to investigate the pattern further:

Row 1: 1 ch, (sc) in 2nd ch and in every ch across, flip

That is, make one chain stitch, skip the first chain away from the hook, then make a single crochet in the second chain away from the hook and each of the remaining 16 chains. Row 1 has now been completed.

Count the stitches carefully, but leave out the loop on the hook and the slip knot at the end of the row. There should be 17 single crochet stitches in total.

Tip: At the end of each row, count the stitches. Most designs will tell you how so many stitches you should use, and there are a few different methods to accomplish that.

- (17 sc).
- 17 sc.
- —17 sc.

These are all examples of how to demonstrate how many stitches you should have. This is not to be confused with a command to accomplish anything.

You've completed your task. 1st Row Look at your pattern: if it says "turn" at the end of a row, it signifies it's time to turn the work so you may continue stitching.

As you turn, always keep the hook in your work.

You are now ready to begin Row 2.

Some designs, however, do not instruct you to turn, ch 1, at the completion of each row. That was written in the next row's instructions.

As a result, the pattern might be written in two ways:

Row 1: 1 ch, (sc) in 2nd ch and in every ch across, flip

Or

Row 1: 1 ch, (sc) in 2nd ch and in every ch across

Row 2; Ch 1, 2 sc in the first sc, sc in every rem sc across to the last sc, 2 sc in the last sc, flip. Row 3: Ch 1, 2 sc in the first sc, and sc in every rem sc across to the last sc, 2 sc in the last sc, flips. (16 sc)

It makes no difference if you work the ch 1, turn at the end of the first row or at the start of the next. Simply follow the pattern's instructions.

Working in Double Crochet

When doing double crochet or higher stitches, there are a few factors to keep in mind:

A dc counts as turning chains.

When starting or turning chains at the beginning of the row ignore the first stitch of the bottom row:

Begin the first row of double crochet, for example.

Ch 13 is written on the pattern.

Row 1: Dc in 4th ch from hook and in each chain across for a total of 10 dc.

So, on the hook, form a slip knot and then 13 chain stitches.

Work a double crochet into the fourth chain away from the hook, skipping the first three chains. Then, in each of the remaining 8 chains, work a double crochet. There are now ten double crochet stitches on your hook.

How is it possible when you've only done ten double crochets? Remember how you skipped the first three chains when doing the first double crochet into the fourth chain from the hook? Those three skipped chains count as the row's initial double crochet, and you'll work into the top chain of those three chains as if it were a regular dc stitch on subsequent rows.

The pattern will inform you how many chain stitches you need to lift the yarn to the level of the stitches for the following row at the end of this row or the beginning of the next. That was one chain in single crochet, and that chain did not qualify as a stitch.

However, to produce double crochet, a higher stitch, make three chains and then turn.

The three chains now count as a stitch. So, on the next row, you'll work into the next stitch rather than the first stitch, assuming that the chain 3 acts as the first dc.

Brackets, Parentheses, And Asterisks

Crochet designs contain various symbols to teach you what to do, in addition to a variety of abbreviations and phrases. A set of steps is commonly repeated numerous times across a row in crochet patterns. Asterisks (*) are used to denote repetitions rather than spelling them out again and again. This is an example of a pattern:

Row 3: Dc in the next 3 sts; *ch 1, omit next st, dc in the next st; rep from * throughout the row (or to end).

That indicates you must repeat the steps after the asterisk in order until you come to the end of the row.

Alternatively, the pattern may state:

Row 3: Ch 1, miss next st, dc in the next st*, rep from * to * throughout row (or repeat between *'s).

That's just another way of expressing the same thing, and you'll follow the steps listed between the two asterisks across the row in order.

To make things even more confusing, you may find yourself repeating processes numerous times in a succession before moving on to anything new! This might imply that you'll discover ** within the *.

A pattern like this may look like this:

Row 3: Ch 1, miss next st, dc in the next st, ** crochet a shell in next st; rep from * throughout row, finishing last rep at **.

Don't scream and fling your hands up in the air! Take each step one at a time. So you'll start with the steps following the asterisk all across row and finish with the **, which means you won't work the shell this time.

Brackets [] are also used to indicate how many times you should repeat a step. The number directly after the brackets indicates how many times you should repeat the procedure.

Consider the following scenario:

Row 7: Dc in the next 4 dc, ch 1, [sk following dc, shell in the next dc] 4 times, ch 1, dc in next 4 dc, ch 1, dc in next 4 dc

That implies you'll repeat [sk next dc, shell in next dc] four times before switching to ch 1, dc in next 4 dc.

In other cases, parentheses are used in the same way.

Parentheses are being used to indicate a set of stitches that will be worked together to form a stitch, for example: in the next dc work (2 dc, ch 3, 2 dc). That implies you'll build a shell by combining all of those stitches into a single dc.

Working in Spaces

It is referring about the "work a puff in the next ch area" (or "in the next arch") command, which is frequently misunderstood by beginners. To construct a chain gap, start with a chain stitch; skip one stitch, and then move on to the next stitch.

You'll need to create the shell in the skipped stitch area (the one beneath the chain). Spaces can be made up of one or more chains; spaces with three or more chains are commonly referred to as loops (lps).

Working in a Round

Many crochet designs, such as granny squares, require crocheters to work in rounds. You should take the following procedures in accordance with the pattern.

To make a ring, chain 6 and attach with a slip stitch.

To achieve this, first form a slip knot on the hook, then make 6 chains, then insert your hook into the first chain, drag your yarn through it, and then through the loop on the hook. As a consequence, you'll have a little circle or ring. You may now add stitches to it.

Loop in the front or back

The bottom row loops are used in the majority of crochet creations. However, some are only formed using the front loop, while others are only made with the back loop. It's important to consider the following when crocheting:

- The nearest loop to you is the front loop.
- The loop that is furthest away from you is called the back loop.

Working Garments

If you're going to make crochet apparel, it's a good idea to learn some of the terminology that is commonly used in the industry:

Right sleeve, right shoulder, and right front: all of these terms refer to bodily portions that the piece will cover, such as the right arm. The same is true for the left sleeve, front, and shoulder.

Incorrect side, right side: Suppose you need to work with the piece's wrong (or right) side facing you. The right side of a garment is the side that will be visible when it is worn.

Right-hand or left-hand Corner: You may be instructed to unite your project's elements at a certain corner. It signifies that the corner of the piece nearest to your left (or right) hand should be joined. At the same time: This implies you must work on two separate processes at the same time (for example, shaping the neckline and armhole).

Work in the same way as the Right (or Left) piece, but reverse the shaping: For novices, this may be rather challenging. On the right sleeve, for example, various reductions have been done. The pattern says: same for the right sleeve, reversing shape, instead of giving directions on how to do it the other way around. That is to say, you will have to find out what to do on your own. It could help for you if you describe what you did at the start on a piece of paper and then work on the other component in the same way but in reverse.

Chapter 4

Basic Crochet Stitches

Chain Stitch

Crocheting is incomplete without chain stitches. Forming a sequence of chain stitches is usually the following step in a project after making a slip knot. Chain stitches serve as the framework for the rest of the project. They are one of a few basic stitches that every learner should be familiar with.

Crochet creations frequently include chain stitches throughout the pattern, in addition to the foundation chain. Chain stitches are used to make stitch patterns, create gaps between patterns, and shape cloth by combining them with other stitches. They can be used as laces for baby booties, decorative thread for tying gifts, and ornament hangers as simple chains.

It takes some practice to keep your tension ideal for chain stitches, but it's a simple stitch to learn.

Instructions

- Holding the Yarn and Hook

Make a slip knot on the hook first. Grab the knot with your left hand's thumb and middle fingers and the slip knot on the crochet hook. You should face the slip knot. The working yarn, the strand that comes from the ball, should run over the index finger, between your middle and index fingers, over your palm, and back to your ring and little fingers. This seems strange at first, but as you construct stitches and will need more yarn from the ball, it will help you tension the yarn.

Use a knife grip, pencil grip, or whatever grip seems most comfortable to you to hold your crochet hook in your hand.

Keep the crochet hooks pointing up to begin. Because you'll be spinning the hook as you form chain stitches, hold it tightly enough to keep control but free enough to move effortlessly.

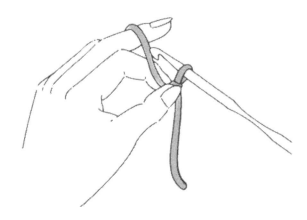

• Yarn Over (YO) the Hook

From back to front, loop the working yarn over (yo) the hook. Wrap the yarn around the crochet hook from the behind and then over the top with your left hand, or manipulate your hook with your right hand to do the same thing. "Yarn over" or "Yarn round hook" are terms used to describe this technique.

• Draw a loop through it

To preparation for hooking, turn your crochet hook one quarter turn counterclockwise while you loop the yarn. It's fine to turn it more if necessary, but the idea is for each move to be as exact and fluid as possible.

• Pull the hook down and then through the loop it is currently in

If you restore the hook to its original position pointing upwards after bringing the yarn through, you will probably find it easier to complete the stitch.

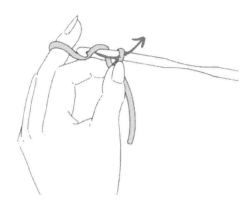

- Creating a Chain

You've just made one chain stitch by "chaining one." Yarn over the hook and draw up a loop to produce another chain stitch. This should be done as many times as needed. Move your index fingers and thumb up the freshly formed chain stitches as you crochet, staying a stitch or two away from the hook loop. This will give you greater control and better tension while stitching: not too tight, nor too loose.

You'll develop a rhythm in which you rotate the crochet hook as you yarn over and then rotate it back as you pull through a loop as you work. Having a routine makes the process go more smoothly and quickly.

Tips for Chain Stitching

- **Counting:** The slip knot isn't usually included in the number of chain stitches required in the foundation chain of a pattern. Your hook's loop isn't any better. Begin counting from your first chain stitch and finish with the chain before the hook.

- **Maintain an even level of tension**: Practice. To learn new abilities, hands require repetition. Your chain stitches will eventually be smooth, even, and not too tight.

- **Modify as needed**: Everyone crochets a little differently, and there are a lot of various methods to hold the yarn and place the hook. One method is demonstrated in these instructions. If this method is inconvenient for you, feel free to change your working style to fit your demands.

- **Don't be afraid to switch hooks**: If you're crocheting with cotton or another non-stretchy yarn, you might need to build your foundation chain using a hook one size larger than the one you'll be using for the rest of the project. Consider beginning anew with a larger hook for the chain if your foundation chain is excessively tight in comparison to the first few rows of stitches that follow it.

SCAN THIS QR CODE TO DOWLOAD THE GRANNY SQUARE EBOOK AND THE FULL COLORED VERSION OF THIS BOOK

Scan me

Single Crochet Stitch

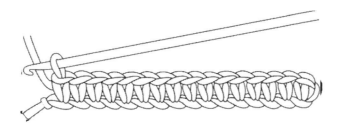

Single crochet is one of the most fundamental stitches to master if you want to learn how to crochet. Single crochet stitches are used in the majority of crochet designs and projects.

One of the simplest stitches to master is single crochet. Once you've mastered the single crochet stitch, you can utilize it in an unlimited number of ways. It may be worked in rows, rounds, or spirals, as an edging, in different areas of the pattern for varied effects, and in limitless combinations with other stitches.

Instructions

- Insert The Crochet Hook

Insert the hook into the first chain of stitches after creating the foundation chain of stitches.

- Slide the crochet hook

Some patterns require you to work over one the loops, resulting in a unique look. If you're unsure, go through both loops.

- Grab the Yarn and Yarn Over

Prepare to make a loop with the crochet hook in place. Wrap the yarn around your crochet hook and pull it tight.

When you've perfected these processes to the point that they're instinctive, you may notice that there's no gap between the first and second steps. As soon as you enter the yarn into the stitch, your hook will grip it.

- Create the Loop

Weaving yarn through the loops while pulling or "drawing" the hook, on your hook, you will then have two stitches or "loops.

- Yarn Over Again

Hook the yarn by wrapping it around your crochet hook once more.

Yarn should be drawn through both loops.

Pull the hook and yarn through the hook's two loops. The single crochet stitch is now complete. On your crochet hook, one loop remains. This loop will be the beginning of your next stitch.

This series of actions can be repeated as many times as necessary to make extra single crochet stitches all across row (or round).

Tips for Beginners

If you're crocheting in rows, the first row, especially for beginners, might be difficult. Many new crocheters struggle to keep their work steady since there isn't much to grasp onto at first.

If you're having problems with the first few rows of single crochet stitch, have an experienced crocheter help you out. After that, you can keep crocheting on the same piece. It will get simpler to hold the work when the first few rows are completed.

After you've worked enough rows to grasp the single crochet stitch, working those tough initial rows in future projects will be much simpler.

Double Crochet Stitch

The double crochet stitch is among the primary stitches that you will learn when you first start crocheting. It's a really adaptable stitch that you may use in a variety of ways throughout your crochet adventure.

- **Start with the foundation chain**

Something to work your double crochet stitches into is required. As a result, you must start by crocheting a foundation chain.

- **Begin by tying a slip knot**

Crochet your chain after that. If you're following a crochet pattern, the pattern will specify the length of your foundation chain.

If you're not using a pattern, crochet a chain that's as long as you want it to be for your project, plus two more stitches. As an example, suppose you wish to crochet a slim scarf with 10 double crochet stitches across it. Create a foundation chain like 10+2 =12

The extra chains are added because they will serve as the first double crochet, as you will see in a moment.

- **Insert Hook into Chain and Yarn Over**

Put the hook into the chain after yarning over it. The hook will be inserted into the third chain from the hook on this initial stitch. Those chains you're skipping act as the row's initial double crochet, though you won't see it until you've finished the following stitch. However, you must add those additional chains to the foundation chain as instructed before in order to make the chains that will constitute the first double crochet.

You may simply believe that this is how you do it for now, so yarn over and place the hook into third chain from the hook.

- **Yarn over again, pulling through**

Pull the yarn through the third chain from the hook at which you put your hook and yarn over again. When you've finished this step, your crochet hook should have three loops.

- **2 loops on hook Yarn over and pull through**

Re-yarn if necessary. Pull the yarn through first two of your hook's three loops. At the end of this stage, the hook will have two loops.

- **Finish the Stitch by Yarning Over**

One last time, re-yarn. Pull both loops that are on the hook through. The double crochet stitch is now complete.

It's as simple as that. When you finish the first double crochet stitch, it should stand to the right of what looks to be another double crochet thread; this is the stitch that was generated when you skipped the first three chains since they function as the first double crochet (dc) stitch of the first row.

The directions in this topic state "to the right" are for right-handed crocheters. For left-handed crocheters, the situation will be the polar opposite.

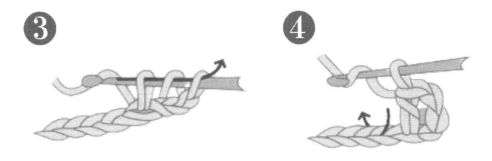

Half Double Crochet

The half double crochet pattern is a lovely crochet stitch that is both basic and flexible. When learning to crochet, a learner should grasp one of the basic crochet stitches. These instructions will teach you how to crochet the half double crochet stitch. This stitch would be a good next step for beginners who have already learned single crochet and double crochet.

HDC is higher than single crochet but shorter than double crochet, as the name implies. It's a fundamental crochet stitch that's done in the same way as the other two. The decreased height and distinctive third loop are the result of a minor variation.

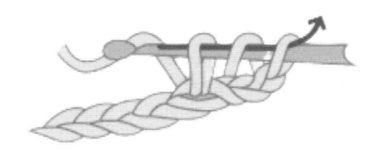

Instructions

- Crochet Hook and Yarn Selection

Because the half double crochet stitch appears in a variety of projects, you can work on it with any yarn and any crochet hook. If you're using a crochet design, the instructions will tell you exactly what materials you'll need.

If you're not following a pattern, choose your yarn and then check the yarn label to see what hook size you'll need. As a starting point, beginners should use worsted-weight yarn and a size H crochet hook.

- Make a foundation chain by crocheting a chain

A slip knot is the starting point for all crochet projects. Then, to work the first row into, build a foundation chain. A foundation chain (also known as a starting chain) can be any length. If you're working with a crochet pattern, follow the instructions for chain length.

- Begin with the correct chain

Crochet into the chain three chains away from your hook to weave the first half double crochet (hdc) into the foundation chain.

You start each row with a turning chain when crocheting in rows. The turning chain's height is determined by the height of the crocheted stitch. Chain two for a turning chain in half double crochet.

- Insert the Crochet Hook and Yarn Over

It's time to start working on the first HDC. Yarn over and into the stitch using the crochet hook.

Note that you would also execute this step if you were creating a double crochet stitch. You just wouldn't yarn over before inserting the crochet hook if you were doing a single crochet stitch. The yarn over increases the stitch's height, making it taller than a single crochet stitch.

- Pull the Yarn Through the Stitch and Yarn Over

Reverse the yarn and draw it through the stitch. On the hook, you should now have three loops.

- Yarn over the loops and pull them through

Reverse the yarn and pull it through all three loops one more time.

The first half double crochet (hdc) stitch is now complete.

- Finish the Row

Working across the foundation chain row and all stitches of each succeeding row, repeat the procedures for each HDC.

Treble Crochet Stitch

After the double crochet, the US triple crochet is the next fundamental stitch in height. It's a common stitch in crochet patterns, and it's usually one of the first stitches that newcomers to the trade learn. The phrases "triple crochet stitch" and "treble crochet stitch" are interchangeable. It will not be hard to learn how to treble crochet if you have already learned how to double crochet.

When a longer stitch, higher than a double crochet but structured on the same design, is required in a crochet design, the treble crochet is utilized. tr is the acronym used in crochet pattern instructions.

Instructions

- Insert hook into the next stitch after yarning over hook twice.
- Draw yarn through stitch using yarn over hook
- Draw through two loops by looping yarn over hook
- Draw two loops through yarn over hook.
- Loop yarn over hook once more and draw through the hook's last two loops.
- One treble crochet is now complete.

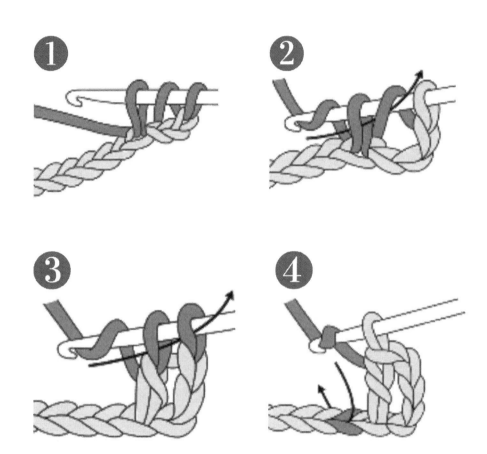

Slip Stitch

A basic crochet stitch which every crocheter needs to know is the slip stitch. It can even be used by knitters. Slip stitch can be used to connect parts, add ornamental components, and finish projects with simple edging.

Because slip stitch is shorter than single crochet, it may be used in patterns as a technique to create a smaller stitch. It's also a versatile stitch with numerous applications.

Slip stitch edging, like the one shown above, can assist smooth the sides or hem of a piece, giving it a more polished appearance. It's customary to stitch this in the same yarn as the rest of the project, but it's also enjoyable to add a pop of contrast!

- Begin working on your slip stitch

A slip stitch can be used at any point once you've started your project.

Insert your crochet hook into the location where you wish to crochet the slip stitch if you already have an active loop on the hook. Then, as shown, hook your yarn.

- Yarn should be pulled through

Pull the yarn through your project and up to the top.

- Complete the Slip Stitch

Finally, draw the newly generated loop through your hook's active loop. After a few tries, these steps become almost one continuous motion. The slip stitching is now finished.

- Joining a Crochet Round or Forming a Ring

Creating a Ring

Some designs, like as granny squares or hexagon patterns, start with a ring in the center. These patterns usually begin with a small number of chain (ch) stitches that are joined to make a ring, and the connection is made with a slip stitch.

Simply place the hook into the edge of the starting chain and slip stitch to produce a ring.

Taking Part in a Round

Slip stitch can be quite useful when crocheting in rounds. You can wind up with a large gap between both the beginning of the round and the conclusion of the round when you complete crocheting a round. A slip stitch can be used to narrow the space between the first and last stitch of a round. When making granny squares, for example, this is frequent.

If you're following a pattern, the pattern will tell you whether or not to perform this. If you're working the rounds in a continuous spiral, for example, a slip stitch isn't always necessary at this point.

Chapter 5

Easy Crochet Patterns

Red Crochet Hearts Pattern

Materials

- Crochet hook 3.5mm
- Yarn
- Yarn needle

Gauge

- 1 Inch = 2 ½ rows

Directions of Pattern

- To form the ring, chain 5 and slip stitch into first chain.
- Round 1: Make a ring with 2 chains and 19 double crochets. With a slip stitch into the head of the first double crochet, join the two pieces together.
- Round 2: Chain 1, then two single crochets (sc) into next two stitches; 1 half double crochet (hdc) into next 3 stitches; 1 double crochet (dc) into next 4 stitches; 3 double crochets (dc) into next stitch (to form the bottom tip of the heart); 1 double crochet (dc) into next 4 stitches; 1 half double crochet (hdc) into next 3 stitches; 2 single crochets (sc) into next 2 stitches Make a slip stitch into the first single crochet to connect. There will be a total of 25 stitches now.
- Round 3: Chain 1 and start making 1 single crochet (sc) in same stitch; 2 half double crochets (hdc) in next stitch; 1 double crochet (dc) in next 4 stitches; 1 half double crochet (hdc) in next 2 stitches; 1 single crochet (sc) in next 4 stitches; 3 single crochets (sc) into next stitch (it should be in the center of the single crochet of 3-single crochet edge of the row at bottom); 1 single crochet (sc) in next 4 stitches; 1 half double crochet (hdc) in next 2 stitches; 1 single crochet (sc) in next 4 stitches; 1 single crochet in next 4 stitches; Make a slip stitch to the first single crochet to connect. There will be a number of 29 stitches now.
- Round 4: Chain 1 and work 1 single crochet into the same stitch; 1 double crochet (dc) into the next stitch; 2 double crochets (dc) into the next 4 stitches; 1 single crochet (sc) into the next 8 stitches; 3 single crochets (sc) into the next stitch (you should be at the edge of the heart); 1 single crochet (sc) into next 8 stitches; 2 double crochets (dc) into the next 4 stitches; 1 double crochet (dc) into next stitch; 1 single crochet (sc) into the next stitch; 1 single crochet (sc) into next stitch; 1 single crochet (sc) into the next stitch Make a slip stitch to the first single crochet to connect. There will be a number of 39 stitches now.

- Round 5: Chain 1 and start making 1 single crochet (sc) into the same stitch; 2 double crochets (dc) into the next 3 stitches, 1 double crochet (dc) into the next stitch; 2 double crochets (dc) into next stitch; 1 double crochet (dc) into the next stitch; 1 double crochet (dc) into the next stitch; 1 double crochet (dc) into next stitch; 1 half double crochet (hdc) into the next 4 stitches; 2 single crochets (sc) into the next stitch; 1 single crochet (sc) into next 7 stitches; 3 single crochets (sc) into the next stitch (you will now be at the edge of the Make a slip stitch to the first single crochet to connect. You'll have a total of 51 stitches at the end.
- Tie a knot in the yarn and pull the extra yarn through the heart.

Simple Slouch Beanie Pattern

Materials

- Crochet hook 5 mm
- Crochet hook 4 mm
- Medium weight yarn
- Tapestry needle

Gauge

14 Double crochets into 9 rows (4 inches)

Directions of Pattern

- Make a magic loop to begin the hat.
- Row 1: Chain 2 (counts as first double crochet), then create 11 double crochets through into ring. Join to the head of chain 2 and tighten the loop (you will end up with 12 stitches).
- Row 2: Chain 2 (this will be your first double crochet), double crochet (dc) into same stitch, *2 double crochets (dc) into next stitch* all the way around, and connect (you will end up with 24 stitches).
- Row 3: Chain 2 (counts as the first double crochet), double crochet (dc) into the next stitch, 2 double crochets in the next stitch, *double crochet (dc) into the next 2 stitches, 2 double crochets (dc) in next stitch*Repeat all the way around, then connect (you will end up with 32 stitches).
- Row 4: Chain 2 (counts as the first double crochet), 2 double crochets (dc) into next stitch, *double crochet (dc) into next 3 stitches, 2 double crochets (dc) into next stitch* Join by repeating from * the entire whole around. (At this point, you should have 40 stitches.)
- Row 5: Chain 2 (counts as first double crochet), 2 double crochets (dc) into next stitch, *double crochet into next 4 stitches, 2 double crochets (dc) into next stitch* Join by repeating from * all the way around. (You'll end up with 48 stitches now.)
- Row 6: Chain 2 (counts as first double crochet), 2 double crochets (dc) into next stitch, *double crochet (dc) into next 5 stitches, 2 double crochets into next stitch* Join by repeating from * all the way around. (You'll end up with 56 stitches now.)
- Row 7: Chain 2 (counts as first double crochet), 2 double crochets (dc) into next stitch, *double crochet into next 6 stitches, 2 double crochets into next stitch* Join by repeating from * all the way around. (You'll end up with 64 stitches now.)
- Row 8: Chain 2 (counts as first double crochet), 2 double crochets (dc) into next stitch, *double crochet (dc) into next 7 stitches, 2 double crochets into next stitch*. Join by repeating from * all the way around. (You'll end up with 72 stitches now.)
- Row 10: Chain 2 and double crochet in each stitch. Join by repeating from * all the way around.
- Rows 10-28: Join and repeat Row 9's pattern.
- You may increase or decrease the number of rows crocheted according on how long you want the droop to be or the tension gauge.
- Change to the smaller hook on row 29. *Single crochet in each stitch only in back loop*, chain 1. Join by repeating from * all the way around.
- Rows 30-34: Repeat Row 29's pattern.
- Tie the yarn in a knot and sew in the loose ends.

Crochet Holiday Pinecones Pattern

Materials

- Tapestry needle
- Cotton yarn
- Crochet hook 5.5 mm

Directions of Pattern

- Begin by making a magic loop in the woods. Round pine cones will be created.
- Round 1: Pull the ring closed with 6 single crochets.
- Round 2: Work 2 single crochets in each single crochet around the whole circle (You will end up with12 single crochets).
- Round 3: * single crochet (sc) into next single crochet * repeat from * around the circle (You will end up with 18 single crochets).
- Round 4: * single crochet (sc) into next two single crochets, increase into next single crochet (sc), repeat pattern * all the way around (You will end up with 24 single crochets).

- Round 5: * single crochet (sc) into the next three single crochets, increase into the next three single crochets, repeat pattern * all the way around (You will end up with 30 single crochets).
- Round 6 a: Slip stitch and chain 3 into one stitch, double crochet into the next, slip stitch into next - 3 stitches* loop pattern * all the way around, chain 1. (You will end up with 10 "petals" and chain 1).
- Round 6 b: *Single crochet into the next 8, reduce once* repeat pattern * all the way around, connect, chain 1 (You will end up with 27 single crochets).
- Single crochet through each single crochet (sc) together all way around in round 7. (You will end with 27 single crochets).
- Round 8 a: Slip stitch and chain 3 within one stitch, double crochet (dc) into the next, slip stitch into next - 3 stitches* loop pattern * all the way around, chain 1. (You will end with 9 "petals" and chain 1).
- Round 8 b: *Single crochet into the next 7, reduce once* repeat the pattern * all the way around, connect, chain 1 (You will end with 24 single crochets).
- Single crochet through each single crochet together all way around in round nine (You will end with 24 single crochets).
- Round 10 a: Slip stitch and chain 3 in one thread, double crochet (dc) into next, slip stitch into the next - 3 stitches* loop pattern * together all way around, chain 1. (You will have now 8 "petals" and chain 1).
- Round 10 b: *Single crochet into the next 6, reduce once* repeat the pattern * all the way around, connect, chain 1 (You will have 21 single crochets).
- Single crochet within every single crochet together all way around in round 11 (You will end with 1 single crochets).
- Round 12 a: Slip stitch and chain 3 through one stitch, double crochet (dc) into the next, slip stitch into next - 3 stitches* repeat pattern * all the way around, chain 1 (You will end with 7 "petals" plus chain 1).
- Round 12 b: *Single crochet into the next 5, reduce once* continue the pattern * all the way around, connect, chain 1 (You will end with 18 single crochets).

- Single crochet (sc) through each single crochet all the way around in round 13 (You will end with 18 single crochet).
- Round 14 a: Slip stitch and chain 3 inside one stitch, double crochet (dc) into next, slip stitch into next - 3 stitches* repeat pattern * all the way around, chain 1 (You will end with 6 "petals" and chain 1).
- 20. Round 14 b: *Single crochet into the next 4, reduce once* continue the pattern * all the way around, connect, chain 1 (You will end with 15 single crochets).
- Single crochet (sc) into each single crochet together all way around in round 15 (You will end with 15 single crochets)
- Round 16 a: Slip stitch and chain 3 through one stitch, double crochet into next, slip stitch into next - 3 stitches* loop pattern * all the way around, chain 1. (You will end with 5 "petals" and chain 1).
- Round 16 b: *single crochet into the next 3, reduce once* duplicate the pattern * together all way around, connect, chain 1 (You will end with 12 single crochets).
- Round 17: Single crochets all the way around into each single crochet (You will end with 12 single crochets).
- Round 18 a: Slip stitch and chain 3 in one thread, double crochet into next, slip stitch into next - 3 stitches* loop pattern * together all way around, chain 1. (You will end with 4 "petals" and chain 1).
- Round 18 b: *Single crochet into the next 2, reduce once* repeat the pattern * all the way around, connect, chain 1 (You will end with 9 single crochets).
- Single crochet through each single crochet together all way around in round 19 (You will end with 9 single crochets). *slip stitch and chain 3 as one stitch, double crochet (dc) into next, slip stitch into next - 3 stitches* replicate the pattern * together all way around in the front loops only (You will now have 3 "petals").
- Cut the yarn and thread the loose ends through.

Jelly Jars Covers Pattern

Materials

- Yarn needle
- Fine yarn
- Jelly jar with a 3" lid
- Crochet hook 3.75mm
- Ribbon 1 meter

Gauge

- 3 Inches = 3 rounds

Directions of Pattern

- To create a ring, crochet three chains and slip stitch the first chain.
- Round 1: Make 11 double crochet (dc) into ring (this will count as the initial double crochet throughout the design). Join the first three chains with a slip stitch in the third chain. There will be a total of 12 double crochets.
- Round 2: Chain 3, double crochet (dc) into round 1's double crochet. Round 1: Make 2 double crochets into each double crochet. Join the first three chains with a slip stitch in the third chain. There will be 24 double crochets in all.

- Chain 3, double crochet (dc) into the same double crochet as in round 2, then double crochet (dc) into the next double crochet. *2 double crochet (dc) in next double crochet, dc in next dc * Repeat * for a total of ten times. Join using a slip stitch in the third chain of the three-chain commencement. You should now have 36 double crochet stitches.
- Round 4: Chain 1 (counts as single crochet), working exclusively in back loop stitch, single chain all the way around. Join using a slip stitch at the start of the first chain. You were supposed to make 36 single chains.
- Rounds 5–7: Chain 1, *miss the next single crochet (sc) and create 2 single crochet in the following single crochet* loop from * around. Make a slip stitch into first single crochet to unite the pieces.
- Round 8 (the eyelet round through which the ribbon will be threaded): Chain 3, *skip 2 single crochets and single crochet into next single crochet, chain 2*. Join using a slip stitch in the first chain of the three chain pattern.
- Round 9: Slip stitch in first chain, leaving 2 spaces, *single crochet (sc), double crochet (db), treble crochet (tb), double crochet (dc), single crochet (sc),* in every 2nd space. * Rep from * around the circle, joining with a slip stitch in first single crochet.
- Tie a knot and snip the yarn.
- Finishing: Using a yarn needle, weave in the loose yarn ends. Tie a bow with the ribbon through the round 8 (the eyelet round).
- Cover the jelly jar with the cover.

Soap Saver Bag Pattern

Materials

- Yarn needle
- Crochet hook 5.0mm
- Cotton yarn (for bag)
- Crochet hook 5.5mm
- Cotton yarn (drawstring)

Gauge

- 1 Inch = 3 rows and 4 stitches

Directions of Pattern

- Crochet 11 chains with the 5.5mm hook.
- Row 1: Single crochet (sc) in the second chain from the hook and each chain across. You'll have ten single crochets now. Turn.
- Row 2: Single crochet in every stitch across the row. There will be ten single crochets in all. Turn.

- Row 3 (here is when you'll start making a circular bag shape): In the initial stitch, chain 1 and do 2 single crochets. Single crochet in each stitch until the row's final stitch, then do a 2 single crochet in the row's last stitch. 3 single crochet along each of the three rows Make two single crochets in the first chain, starting at the bottom ends of the original chain. Single crochet (sc) in each chain till you reach the last chain, then double crochet in that chain. Join in the first single chain with 3 single crochet up from the side of the rows. Don't turn since you'll end up with a circular form. There will be a total of 30 stitches.
- Row 4: Chain 4 (double chain with single chain) and omit the next stitch *double crochet (dc) into the next stitch, chain 1, and skip the following stitch** in a circular pattern, repeat the directions from * to **. At the top of the rotating chain, join together. There should be 15 double crochet stitches in total.
- Round 5: Create 4 chains (double chain in chain 1 and create spaces with 1 chain**), *double chain in chain 1 and create spaces with 1 chain**. Rep from * to ** all the way around. At the top of the rotating chain, join the round. A total of 15 double crochet stitches will be used.
- Rounds 6–9: repeat round 5 with the same method.
- Round 10: Make 1 chain, half double crochet (hdc) in each chain, leaving 1 gap, then double crochet all the way around. Leave a tail on the yarn and connect using an invisible join. (Throw the tail through to the yarn needle and pull through the last stitch with the needle.) Insert the needle into the next stitch's chain and pull it through. Continue until the entire tail has been inserted.
- Drawstring: Make a compact chain of 70 chains with the 5.0 hook. Leave a tail by pulling the yarn through the last chain. Start weaving the drawstring using the top half double crochets formed in round 10 by threading the tail through the yarn needle. Tie the two ends together with a knot and cut the loose yarn.
- Pull the drawstring closed and fill the bag with the final pieces of soap from the bar.

Chapter 6

Modern Crochet Patterns

Bucket Hat Pattern

Materials

- 5.5 mm hook
- Felici Worsted Yarn
- Stitch Marker

Gauge

- 8 rows = 2 in
- 8 sts = 2 in

Directions of Pattern

- Begin by getting a magical ring. (or make a ring by ch 4 and sl st into the first ch)
- Round 1: 6 sc into the ring (ch 1, 6 sc into ring).
- 2 sc for each st around in round 2.
- Round 3: (Sc, 2 sc next) all the way around.
- Round 4: (Sc in next 2 sts, 2 sc in next) all the way around.
- Round 5: (Sc in next 3 sts, 2 sc in next) all the way around.
- Round 6: (Sc in next 4 sts, 2 sc in next sts) all the way around.
- Round 7: (Sc for each of the next 5 sts, 2 sc in each of the following 2 sts) around.
- Round 8: (Sc in next 6 sts, 2 sc in next) all the way around.
- Round 9: (Sc in next 7 sts, 2 sc in next) all the way around.
- (Sc in next 8 sts, 2 sc for the next) around in round 10.
- (Sc in next 9 sts, 2 sc in next) around in round 11.
- Round 12: (Sc in next 10 sts, 2 sc in next) all the way around.
- Round 13: (Sc in next 11 sts, 2 sc in next) all the way around.
- Fl sl st for each st around in round 14.
- 14.5th round: (Working in the backside loops of row 14) sc for each st around with a bl sc.
- Sc for each st around in rounds 15-27.
- Fl sc for each st around on round 28.
- (Sc in next 5 sts, 2 sc in next) around in round 29.
- (Sc over the next 6 sts, 2 sc in next) around in round 30.
- Sc for each st around in rounds 31-32.
- 33rd round: (Sc in next 7 sts, 2 sc in next)
- Sc for each st around in round 34.
- (Sc in next 8 sts, 2 sc over the next) around in round 35.
- Sc for each st around in rounds 36-38.
- Fasten off.

Crochet Throw Pattern

Materials

- Any bulky (5) yarn
- Scissors
- Crochet Hook Size 6 mm
- Yarn needle

Gauge

- 10 sts x 6 rows = 4"

Directions of Pattern

- Row 1: sc in second ch from hook, sc in each st across 34 (85, 103, 115, 133,175,235,274; 85, 103, 115, 133,175,235,274)
- Row 2: ch 3, make a dc in the first st, *skip 2 st's, dc 3 times in the next st, repeat from* through, finishing with 3 st's, skip 2 and 2 dc's in final st, turn. (When counting sts, the turning chains are counted as a dc in these rows.)
- Row 3: ch 1, make a sc in first st, sc in each st across, sc in final st, turn (or the top of the turning chain). 34. (85, 103, 115,133,175,235,274)
- Row 4: ch 3, make a dc in first st, *skip 2 st's, dc 3 times in the next st, repeat from* through, finishing with 3 st's, skip 2 and 2 dc in final st, turn (when counting these rows, the turning chains are counted as stitches.)
- Row 5: repeat row 3
- Row 6: repeat the rows from the previous rows.
- Row 7: continue row 3&4 to the row of the blanket size you're constructing from the chart above.
- Finishing: Using a yarn needle, weave in loose ends throughout the project.

Crochet Granny Pillow Pattern

Materials

- Any bulky (5) yarn
- Scissors
- Crochet Hook Size 6 mm
- Yarn needle

Directions of Pattern

- Chain 5 or make a magic ring by joining the first and last chains with a slip stitch in the first chain. 3rd chain (this is first dc). 1 dc + 1 ch * rep for another 8 times. In the first dc you formed at the start of this row, make 1 slip stitch. Change the color scheme.
- 1 sl st + 3 ch (= the very first dc) in the following chain-1-space. In the same chain-1-space, make 1 dc. Chain 1. * 2 dc in next chain-1-space, chain 1. * 2 dc in next chain-1-space, chain 1. * 2 dc in next chain-1-space, reverse the process. In the first dc you formed at the start of this row, make 1 slip stitch. Change the color scheme.

- 1 sl st + 3 ch (= the very first dc) in the following chain-1-space. In the same chain-1-space, make two dcs. * 3 dc in the following chain-1-space, chain 1. * reverse the process. In the first dc you formed at the start of this row, make 1 slip stitch. Change the color scheme.
- 1 sl st + 3 ch (= the very first dc) in the following chain-1-space. Chain 1, 2 dc in the very same chain-1-space, chain 1. * 2 dc in following chain-1-space, chain 1, 2 dc in same chain-1-space, chain 1. * 2 dc in same chain-1-space, chain 1. Reverse the process. In the first dc you formed at the start of this row, make 1 slip stitch. Change the color scheme.
- 1 sl st + 3 ch (= the very first dc) in the following chain-1-space. In the same chain-1-space, make two dcs. * 3 dc in the following chain-1-space, chain 1. * reverse the process. In the first dc you formed at the start of this row, make 1 slip stitch. Change the color scheme.
- 1 sl st + 3 ch (= the first dc) in the following chain-1-space. In the same chain-1-space, make two dcs. * 3 dc in the following chain-1-space, chain 1. * reverse the process. In the first dc you formed at the start of this row, make 1 slip stitch. Change the color scheme.
- 1 sl st + 3 ch (= the very first dc) in the following chain-1-space. Chain 1, 2 dc in same ch-1-space, ch 1. * 2 dc within next chain-1-space, ch 1, 2 dc in the very same chain-1-space, chain 1. * 2 dc in the same chain-1-space, chain 1. Reverse the process. In the first dc you formed at the start of this row, make 1 slip stitch. Change the color scheme.
- 1 sl st + 3 ch (= the very first dc) in the following chain-1-space. In the same chain-1-space, make 1 dc. Chain 1. * 2 dc in the chain-1-space after that, chain 1. * reverse the process. In the first dc you formed at the start of this row, make 1 slip stitch. Change the color scheme.
- 1 SL st + 3 ch (= the very first dc) in the following chain-1-space. In the same chain-1-space, make two dcs. * 3 dc in the following chain-1-space, chain 1. * reverse the process. In the first dc you formed at the start of this row, make 1 slip stitch. Change the color scheme.
- 1 sl st + 3 ch (= the very first dc) in the following chain-1-space. In the same chain-1-space, make two dcs. * 3 dc in the following chain-1-space, chain 1. * reverse the process. In the first dc you formed at the start of this row, make 1 slip stitch. Change the color scheme.

- 1 sl st + 3 ch (= the very first dc) in the following chain-1-space. In the same chain-1-space, make two dcs. * 3 dc in the following chain-1-space, chain 1. * reverse the process. In the first dc you formed at the start of this row, make 1 slip stitch. Change the color scheme.
- 1 st + 3 ch (= the very first dc) in the following chain-1-space. In the same chain-1-space, make two dcs. * 3 dc in the following chain-1-space, chain 1. * reverse the process. In the first dc you formed at the start of this row, make 1 slip stitch. Change the color scheme.
- 1 st + 3 ch (= the very first dc) in the following chain-1-space. Chain 1, 2 dc in same ch-1-space, ch 1. * 2 dc in the next ch-1-space, ch 1, 2 dc in same ch-1-space, ch 1. * 2 dc in same chain-1-space, chain 1. Reverse the process. In the first dc you formed at the start of this row, make 1 slip stitch. Change the color scheme.
- 1 SL st + 3 ch (= the very first dc) in the following chain-1-space. In the same chain-1-space, make 1 dc. Chain 1. * 2 dc in the chain-1-space after that, chain 1. * reverse the process. In the first dc you formed at the start of this row, make 1 slip stitch. Change the color scheme.
- 1 SL st + 3 ch (= the very first dc) in the following chain-1-space. In the same chain-1-space, make 1 dc. Chain 1. * 2 dc in the chain-1-space after that, chain 1. * reverse the process. In the first dc you formed at the start of this row, make 1 slip stitch. Change the color scheme.
- 1 SL st + 3 ch (= the very first dc) in the following chain-1-space. In the same chain-1-space, make 1 dc. Chain 1. * 2 dc in the chain-1-space after that, chain 1. * reverse the process. In the first dc you formed at the start of this row, make 1 slip stitch. Finish by tying off and removing the yarn ends.

Water Bottle Cozy Pattern

Materials

- Yarn
- Hook: Size H, 5.0mm
- Yarn Needle
- Button 3/4" or 1"
- Scissors
- Stitch Markers

Gauge

- 15 hdc by 11 rows (4")

Directions of Pattern

- 10 hdc in circle – 10 sts R1: Ch 1, 10 hdc in round – 10 sts
- 2 hdc for each st around – 20 Sts. R2: 2 hdc within every st around – 20 Sts.
- R3: *Hdc 1, 2 hdc in the next stitch, repeat * around – 30 stitches
- R4: Sc next, sl st next, ch 1, hdc in BLO of the each st around – 30 stitches
- R5: Hdc around in each st – 30 sts
- You'll be joining the following several rounds to keep the color changes even.
- R6: Sc in next st, sl st in next st, ch 1, hdc in the same and next 29 sts, connect to first hdc, change to colored yarn – 30 sts
- R7: Change to black yarn and ch 1, sc in the same and each st around, connect to first sc – 30 sts
- R8: Ch 1, hdc in the same and that each st around, connect to first hdc with color yarn – 30 sts
- Finish the black and weave in the ends. You'll be back to working in the circle in no time. To keep track of the rows, use a stitch marker.

Front and Back Fingerless Mittens

Materials

- US H/8 (5mm) hook
- US I/9 (5.5mm) hook
- Yarn
- Yarn needle
- Scissors
- Stitch marker

Gauge

- 11 rows and 16 sts = 4 inches

Directions of Pattern

- Join with a SL st to the top of the first hdc, being careful not to twist the stitches. (26 sts [30 sts])
- 1st and 2nd rounds: ch 2 (gets counted as BPdc), FPdc in the next st, *BPdc in the next st, FPdc in the next st; rep from * around. Join with a sl st to the top of the second ch. (26 sts [30 sts])
- Hand: From here on out, work in a continuous spiral with the bigger hook in an alternate (hdcFL, hdcBL) stitch pattern, not joining between rounds. Remember using a stitch marker during first stitch of each round to keep track of your progress.

- Rnd 3: ch 1, sc2tog in FL of first 2 sts, *hdcBL in the next st, hdcFL in the next st; rep from * around with bigger hook. (25 sts [29 sts])
- Rnd 4: hdcBL in the next st, *hdcFL in the next st, hdcBL in the next st; repeat from * all the way around. (25 sts [29 sts])
- Rnd 5: hdcFL in the next st, *hdcBL in the next st, hdcFL in the next st; repeat from * all the way around. (25 sts [29 sts])
- Rep Rnd 6 4th round (25 [29] sts) Increases for the thumb flap should begin now:
- Rnd 7: FBinc in the next 2 sts, hdcFL in the next st, *hdcBL in the next st, hdcFL in the following st; rep from * around. (27 sts [31 sts])
- Rnd 8: hdcBL in the next st, FBinc in the following 2 sts, *hdcFL in the next st, hdcBL in the next st; rep from * throughout. (29 sts [33 sts])
- Rnd 9: hdcFL in the next st, hdcBL in for next st, FBinc in next 2 sts, FBinc in the next 2 sts, hdcFL in the next st, *hdcBL in for next st, hdcFL in the next st; rep from * around (35 [31] stitches)
- Rnd 10: hdcBL in for the next st, hdcFL in the next st, hdcBL in the next st, FBinc in next 2 sts, hdcFL in the next st, hdcBL in the next st, FBinc in for next 2 sts, *hdcFL in the next st, hdcBL in the next st; rep from * throughout. (37 [33] stitches)
- FBinc in the next 2 sts, hdcFL in the next st, *hdcBL in the next st, hdcFL in the next st; rep from * around.
- FBinc in the next 2 sts, hdcFL in the next st, *hdcBL in the next st, hdcFL in the next st; rep from * around. (35 sts [39 sts])
- *hdcBL in the next st, hdcFL in the next st; rep from * through to last st, hdcBL in the next st, hdcFL in the same st (36 sts [40 sts])
- Continue with the hand after leaving the thumb hole:
- HdcBL in the next st, hdcFL in the same st, hdcBL in the next st, *hdcFL in the next st, hdcBL in the next st; rep from * around. (27 sts [31 sts])
- Rnd 16: hdcFL in the next st, *hdcBL in the next st, hdcFL in the next st, hdcFL in the next st; rep from * around. (27 sts [31 sts])
- Rnd 17: hdcBL in the next st, *hdcFL in the next st, hdcBL in the next st, hdcBL in the next st; rep from * round. (27 sts [31 sts])
- Rep Round 16 in Rnd 18. (27 [31] sts)
- sc in BL of the next st, sl st in next st, sc in BL of the next st, sl st in next st, sc in BL of next st, sc (2 stitches plus 25 [29] unworked stitches)
- Fasten off and weave in the yarn tail (if desirable, add an invisible finish in the following stitch to produce a neater connection).
- Close the gap at the base of the cuff with the long beginning tail and a yarn needle, hiding the beginning ch 3 from the chainless foundation inside of the cuff. Weave in the last of the yarn tails.

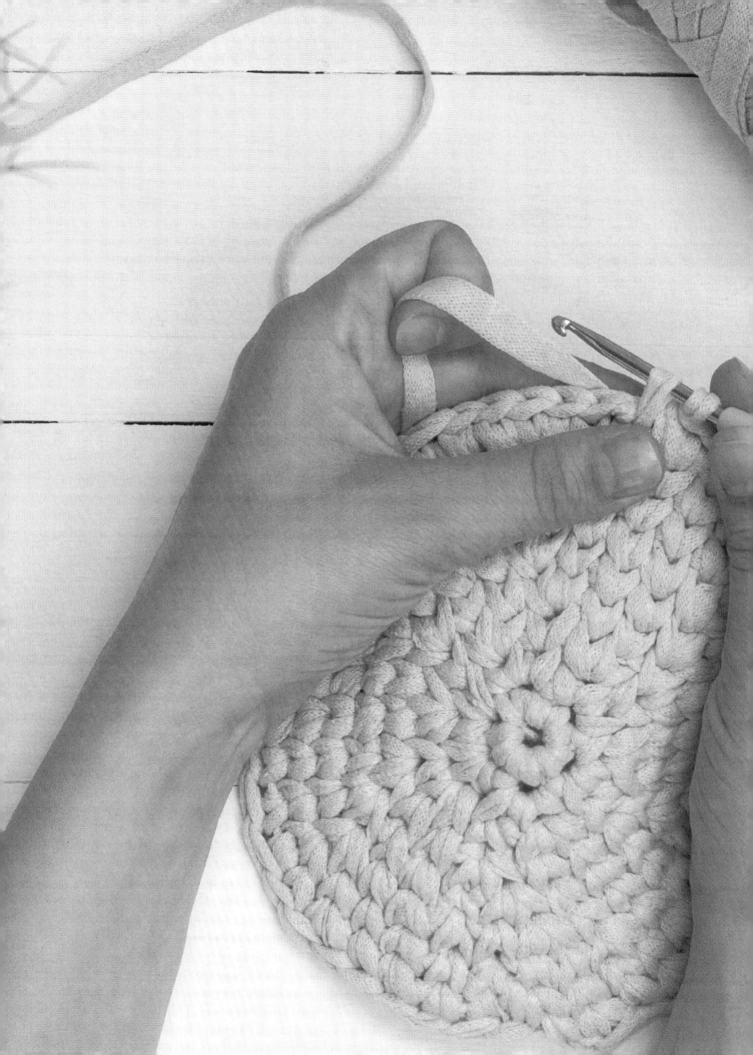

Chapter 7

Tips and Tricks

Before You Begin Crocheting, Turn Your Skeins Into Yarn Balls.

If you're eager to get started on your project, you may be tempted to pull the label off the skein of yarn and begin crocheting. Technically, you can crochet using skeins of yarn, but in many situations, taking the effort to wrap the skein into a ball first can yield superior results. This is particularly true for beginners. Compared to skeins, yarn balls offer a few advantages:

Tangles should be avoided at all costs. Yarn skeins that are pulled from the center can tangle easily at the end. Yarn balls are less prone to tangling.

Increase the level of tension. If you're having trouble getting even tension, consider working with a ball of yarn instead of a skein.

You may use ball winders to assist you with this process, but you can also do by hand.

Before You Begin Crocheting, Remove Any Obstacles

Long hair: If you have long hair that will get through the way of your crocheting, make sure it is combed and tied back before you begin. This keeps your hair from becoming knotted while you're working.

Before you start crocheting, you should take off any jewelry you have on, especially rings and bracelets. Yarn might tangle with jewelry and obstruct your progress.

Keep cats out of the area when you're crocheting if at all feasible. A cat can't seem to stay away from a spinning ball of yarn. A crochet creation may also be easily ruined by a cat.

Arrange the Yarn Properly

Place the ball of yarn in such a way that it can simply unravel as you crochet.

If you're crocheting at home in a cozy chair, you can position the ball of yarn in your lap or at your feet, depending on your preference.

Put the ball of yarn inside a tote if you're crocheting on an airplane or in a moving vehicle to keep it from spinning around and unwinding.

When It's Time to Switch Crochet Hooks, Do So

Crocheters who are new to the craft have a tendency to work too loosely or too tightly. Choose a bigger crochet hook if your work is too tight. Select a smaller crochet hook if your work is too loose.

Please remember that the hook size listed on the yarn label is only a guideline. Experiment with hooks before beginning a project. When you're producing gauge swatches, now is the best time to do so.

Switching Hooks in Between Project Is a Bad Idea

Throughout your project, you want the stitches to remain constant. You run the risk of causing inconsistencies if you swap hooks. Even little differences in hook size from one manufacturer to the next might be troublesome. Manufacturers do not always use the same hook size.

The way you grip the hook or create your stitches may be affected by minor changes in hook shape.

Crochet Hooks That Are Ergonomic

Ergonomic crochet hooks are made to be as comfortable as possible. If you can locate an ergonomic hook that you like, it may make your crocheting time more pleasurable than it otherwise would be.

Make Gauge Swatches

You might be tempted to assume that crocheting gauge swatches is pointless. It's the most important aspect of the project, especially if it's a garment. If you ignore the gauge swatch, your project will almost certainly be too small.

Do Not Be Afraid to Unravel

If you make a mistake a few rows back, tear out the stitches up until that point and start over.

Don't Be Afraid To Try New Techniques and Experiments

There are no "crochet cops," and if an experiment fails, nothing bad will happen to you. Experimentation and practice are two of the most effective strategies to go past the novice stage. Consider the following examples of small experiments:

- Change the colors in a pattern.
- Various yarn selections.
- Details can be added or subtracted: If a design calls for fringe, use an edge instead, or add a flower to a plain hat.

Don't be scared to perform more difficult experiments as you gain more knowledge:

- To make a simple design more interesting, add stripes.
- Use a variety of stitches.
- Customize a sweater by adding long sleeves rather than short sleeves and changing the collar.

Although some of these experiments may fail, each one will educate you something new.

Make Friends with Other Crocheters

You've undoubtedly worked out that there are a lot of different ways to crochet, and they're all valid. Crocheters who have been doing it for a long time have a wealth of knowledge and experience to give.

Join a local crochet club or look for a forum where you may learn more from these seasoned professionals. Even if you've been into craft of crocheting for a long time, there's always something new to learn.

Conclusion

The stronger you are at basic abilities it will be better to produce things, like with any craft. It's essential for a beginner to grasp the many types of materials, how they affect the final creation, and the vocabulary used by other crafters to explain the process.

Crocheting is a soothing hobby. Not only that, but you can make some fantastic items, like as toys and sweaters. Enjoy designing crochet designs, which will allow you to supplement your income. It also keeps one's hands occupied while watching TV, which is beneficial if you're prone to snacking while watching. Crocheting for a Cause is a fun way to learn new techniques and designs while helping others by crocheting Afghans, toques, and other warm things. Whatever the reason, you will gain satisfaction from knowing that you have improved someone's life.

Learning to crochet will be a great project to embark on. Crochet is a great and simple method to express you. Allow your imagination to go wild. Your crocheted items may not be as flawless as you'd like them to be at first, but with experience, you'll be able to create stunning necklaces, bracelets, and bags.

SCAN THIS QR CODE TO DOWLOAD THE GRANNY SQUARE EBOOK AND THE FULL COLORED VERSION OF THIS BOOK

Scan me

Amigurumi for Beginners

Chapter 1: Introduction

Welcome to the enchanting world of amigurumi, a craft that transcends the boundaries of crochet and transforms simple yarn into whimsical characters, cuddly creatures, and charming treasures. In this introductory chapter, we'll embark on a journey into the heart of amigurumi, exploring its magic, allure, and the unique path we will traverse together through the pages of this book.

The Enchantment of Amigurumi

Amigurumi, a term originating from Japan that combines "ami" (crocheted or knitted) and "nuigurumi" (stuffed doll), is a craft like no other. It's more than just creating soft toys; it's about weaving stories, infusing life into yarn, and bringing smiles to faces. The charm of amigurumi lies not only in the finished product but in the process of crafting it.

Why Amigurumi?

You may wonder what makes amigurumi stand out amid the vast world of crafting. Let's dive into the compelling reasons why amigurumi has become a beloved art form for crafters around the globe.

1. Creative Expression: A Canvas for Imagination

Amigurumi offers a unique canvas for creative expression. It's a world where you can translate your imagination into tangible creations. From designing adorable animals to reimagining beloved characters, each amigurumi project is a reflection of your artistic vision. With every stitch, you breathe life into your creations.

2. Handmade Treasures in a Mass-Produced World

In an era dominated by mass-produced goods, amigurumi stands as a testament to the value of handmade treasures. Each amigurumi piece is a labor of love, crafted with care, and infused with individuality. When you create an amigurumi, you're not just making a toy; you're producing a unique, one-of-a-kind work of art.

3. Crafting Memories

Amigurumi is not just about creating physical items; it's about crafting memories. The process of selecting colors, manipulating yarn, and watching your project evolve becomes an adventure worth remembering. Whether you're gifting your amigurumi to a loved one or keeping it for yourself, the process itself is a cherished memory.

4. Nurturing Creativity

Amigurumi nurtures creativity. As you take on new patterns, experiment with different yarns, and explore intricate techniques, your creative spirit flourishes. This craft challenges you to push boundaries, try new things, and evolve as an artist. It's a journey of growth and discovery.

5. Therapeutic Benefits of Crochet

The rhythmic and repetitive motions of crochet, combined with the focus required for intricate details, create a therapeutic and meditative experience. Crafting amigurumi can be a source of relaxation and stress relief. It's a calming, soothing, and centering activity that allows you to lose yourself in the flow of creativity.

6. Gifting with Heart

When you gift an amigurumi creation, you're not just offering a toy; you're sharing a piece of yourself. The recipient can feel the love and care that went into every stitch. Amigurumi gifts are not merely objects; they are tokens of affection, gestures of kindness, and vessels of emotion.

7. Connection and Community

Engaging in amigurumi introduces you to a vibrant and welcoming community of like-minded crafters. Online forums, social media groups, and local events dedicated to this art form provide opportunities to connect, share, and learn from fellow enthusiasts. The sense of belonging and camaraderie adds an enriching dimension to your amigurumi journey.

8. Eco-Conscious Crafting

As we'll explore in more detail later in this book, amigurumi can be an eco-conscious craft. By choosing sustainable materials, recycling yarn, and embracing the principles of responsible crafting, you can create with a conscience. Amigurumi is not just about making cute toys; it's about making them with a mindful commitment to environmental well-being.

9. Playful Joy for All Ages

Finally, amigurumi is about pure, unadulterated joy. The delight that comes from holding a small, crocheted friend in your hands is something that transcends age. Whether you're creating for children or the child within, amigurumi brings smiles, laughter, and happiness.

This book is your portal to the enchanting world of amigurumi. Our journey together will be a transformative one, guiding you through the fundamentals of crochet, the art of reading patterns, and the exhilaration of creating your own amigurumi from scratch. As we continue, you'll discover that amigurumi is not just a craft; it's a joyful, fulfilling, and heartwarming art form that has the power to touch lives and kindle a lasting love for creativity. Are you ready to unlock the magic of amigurumi? Our adventure begins with the basics of crochet. In Chapter 2, we will explore the essential tools and techniques that will pave the way for your amigurumi journey. So, grab your crochet hook, collect your favorite yarn, and let's dive into this world of creativity and craftsmanship together.

Chapter 2: Crochet Basics: Tools and Techniques

Welcome to the foundation of your amigurumi journey. In this chapter, we will delve into the fundamental building blocks of crochet. Whether you're a seasoned crocheter or brand new to the craft, we'll cover everything you need to know about the tools and techniques that will pave the way for your amigurumi adventures.

The Essential Tools

Before you embark on your crochet journey, let's explore the indispensable tools that will be your constant companions as you create your amigurumi masterpieces.

1. Crochet Hooks

The crochet hook is your primary tool, the magic wand that transforms yarn into intricate stitches. These come in various sizes, denoted by a letter or number. For amigurumi, we typically use smaller hook sizes, often ranging from 2.25mm (B/1) to 3.5mm (E/4). The choice of hook size depends on the yarn thickness and your personal tension.

2. Yarn

Selecting the right yarn is paramount to your amigurumi's success. Opt for a smooth, non-fuzzy yarn in your chosen colors. Acrylic and cotton yarns are popular choices due to their ease of use and wide color range. Light worsted or worsted weight yarn is commonly used in amigurumi. Keep in mind, eco-conscious choices include recycled or organic yarns.

3. Scissors

Sharp, small scissors are a must for snipping yarn and thread. Keep them handy in your crafting kit.

4. Yarn Needle

A yarn needle with a large eye is essential for weaving in loose ends and sewing parts of your amigurumi together. Plastic or metal needles work well.

5. Stitch Markers

Stitch markers are small, often removable, clips or rings used to mark specific stitches or locations in your work. They are particularly handy when working in the round.

6. Safety Eyes and Noses (Optional)

For amigurumi projects that require facial features, safety eyes and noses provide a secure and professional finish. These come in various sizes, styles, and colors, adding character to your creations.

7. Fiberfill or Stuffing

To give your amigurumi its soft, cuddly shape, you'll need fiberfill or stuffing material. This fluff, when strategically added, transforms your flat crochet pieces into 3D forms.

8. Optional Embellishments

Depending on your design, you may want to explore embellishments like beads, ribbons, or felt for additional details and decoration.

Understanding Crochet Stitches

Now that you're acquainted with the tools, let's dive into the core of crochet - stitches. At the heart of any crochet project are a handful of basic stitches that form the foundation for more complex patterns. Here are the fundamental crochet stitches you'll encounter in your amigurumi journey:

1. Slip Knot (SK)

Every crochet project begins with a slip knot. To make one, create a loop with your yarn, tuck the working end through the loop, and pull tight. This slip knot is placed on your crochet hook.

2. Chain (CH)

The chain stitch is the most basic of all crochet stitches. To create a chain, wrap the yarn around your hook and pull it through the loop on your hook. Chains serve as the foundation for all crochet work, allowing you to build height and structure.

3. Single Crochet (SC)

The single crochet stitch is short and tight, perfect for creating amigurumi. Insert your hook into a stitch, yarn over, pull up a loop, yarn over again, and pull through both loops on your hook.

4. Double Crochet (DC)

The double crochet stitch is taller than the single crochet. Yarn over, insert your hook into a stitch, yarn over, pull up a loop, yarn over again, pull through the first two loops, then yarn over once more and pull through the remaining two loops.

5. Magic Ring (MR) or Magic Circle

The magic ring is a technique often used in amigurumi to create a tight, closed circle at the beginning of your work. This method allows for a neater starting point than a traditional chain loop.

6. Increase (INC) and Decrease (DEC)

In amigurumi, you'll frequently encounter increases and decreases. Increasing involves working two stitches into the same stitch, while decreasing combines two stitches into one. These techniques create the shaping needed for your amigurumi's form.

7. Slip Stitch (SL ST)

The slip stitch is used to join rounds or create a seamless finish. It's also commonly used to move your hook to a different location in your work.

8. Fasten Off

When you've completed your crochet piece, you'll need to fasten off. Cut your yarn, leaving a tail, and pull it through the final loop on your hook to secure your work.

With your tools and basic stitches in hand, you're equipped to begin your amigurumi journey. In the second part of this chapter, we will delve deeper into the crochet techniques used in amigurumi, such as working in the round, creating different shapes, and increasing and decreasing strategically to shape your creations. Get ready to bring your amigurumi to life with these essential techniques.

Working in the Round

Amigurumi is often worked in a continuous spiral, meaning you won't turn your work at the end of each round. To start, you use a magic ring or chain, and then you work your stitches in a continuous circle. This technique creates a seamless and tidy finish, which is essential for amigurumi's smooth, rounded forms.

Creating Different Shapes

Amigurumi is all about forming various shapes that come together to build your character. You'll often use increases (INC) and decreases (DEC) to shape your work. Here's how they work:

Increase (INC): To make your work wider, work two stitches into the same stitch from the previous round. For example, if you've been working single crochet stitches, you'd work 2 single crochets into the same stitch in the new round. INC stitches are usually spaced throughout the round, gradually shaping your piece.

Decrease (DEC): To make your work narrower, you'll need to decrease stitches. This involves combining two stitches into one. For single crochet, insert your hook into the first stitch, yarn over, pull up a loop, then insert your hook into the next stitch, yarn over, pull up a loop, and then yarn over and pull through all loops on the hook. DEC stitches are used to create curves and angles in your amigurumi.

Changing Colors

Amigurumi often requires changing colors to create intricate patterns or character details. To switch colors, work the last stitch of the old color as usual until you have two loops on your hook. Then, finish the stitch by pulling through with the new color. You can carry the unused color inside your stitches to avoid cutting and weaving in the ends excessively.

Creating Limbs and Features

To craft limbs or add facial features to your amigurumi, you'll need to make separate pieces. For instance, arms and legs are often made as tubes by crocheting rounds of stitches. Features like eyes, noses, and mouths can be created by crocheting tiny shapes or by using other crafting materials like safety eyes and noses.

Weaving in Ends

One of the essential finishing touches for any crochet project is weaving in your ends. After you've completed your amigurumi piece, you'll likely have loose yarn ends from changing colors and fastening off. Thread these ends onto a yarn needle and weave them back into your work, securing them in the stitches. This ensures your amigurumi remains intact and neat.

Blocking Your Amigurumi

While blocking is more common in other crochet projects like blankets and garments, you can use a light blocking technique to shape your amigurumi. It involves gently dampening your amigurumi, shaping it as desired, and letting it dry in the desired shape. This helps achieve a more polished and professional look for your creations.

With these crochet techniques under your belt, you're well on your way to creating beautiful amigurumi. In the chapters to come, we will put these skills to use, guiding you through the process of crafting various amigurumi characters and sharing tips and tricks to make your journey even more enjoyable.

The world of amigurumi is filled with endless possibilities and creative potential. In the next chapter, we'll delve into the heart of amigurumi - the patterns. You'll learn to decipher patterns, understand their components, and gain the confidence to tackle a wide array of amigurumi projects. Get ready to bring your imagination to life one stitch at a time.

Chapter 3: Getting Started with Amigurumi

Congratulations on mastering the crochet basics! You've learned about the essential tools, the core stitches, and the techniques that form the foundation of amigurumi. Now, we're ready to take the next step in your amigurumi journey and dive into the heart of the craft.

Understanding Amigurumi Patterns

Amigurumi patterns are your guiding light in creating these charming creatures. A typical amigurumi pattern includes instructions for each piece, such as the body, arms, legs, and any additional details. Here's how to navigate and understand amigurumi patterns:

1. Materials List

Each pattern will begin with a list of materials you need, such as the type and color of yarn, crochet hook size, safety eyes or other embellishments, and any additional tools required. Review the materials list to ensure you have everything you need before starting.

2. Abbreviations

Amigurumi patterns use crochet abbreviations to save space and make instructions more concise. Common abbreviations you'll encounter include:

SC: Single Crochet

INC: Increase (work two single crochets in the same stitch)

DEC: Decrease (combine two single crochets into one)

CH: Chain

MR: Magic Ring (or Magic Circle)

SL ST: Slip Stitch

BLO: Back Loop Only

FLO: Front Loop Only

Familiarize yourself with these abbreviations to better understand the pattern instructions.

3. Gauge

Some patterns may include a gauge measurement to ensure your stitches are the correct size. Gauge is often not as critical in amigurumi as it is in other crochet projects, but it's useful to check to ensure your finished amigurumi isn't too loose or too tight.

4. Special Techniques

Patterns may introduce special techniques like color changes, creating texture with front loop/back loop only stitches, and instructions for attaching safety eyes and other embellishments. Pay attention to these details as they add character to your amigurumi.

5. Step-by-Step Instructions

The heart of the pattern lies in the step-by-step instructions for each piece of your amigurumi. These instructions will guide you through every stitch, increase, decrease, and color change needed to create your character. Read through these instructions carefully, following each step in sequence.

6. Assembly

Most patterns include instructions on how to assemble your amigurumi, which involves sewing pieces together, attaching safety eyes and noses, and stuffing your creation with fiberfill.

7. Tips and Notes

Patterns often include tips, notes, and photos to clarify any challenging steps or offer suggestions for customizing your amigurumi.

Reading Patterns

Reading amigurumi patterns can seem daunting at first, but with practice, it becomes easier. As you work through more patterns, you'll develop a keen understanding of the structure and logic behind them. Here's a simplified example of a pattern for an amigurumi ball:

Materials:

- Worsted weight yarn in three colors: A, B, and C

- 3.5mm crochet hook

- Fiberfill stuffing

Body:

Round 1: With color A, make a MR and SC 6 into the ring. (6)

Round 2: INC in each SC around. (12)

Round 3: (SC, INC) six times. (18)

Round 4: SC in each SC around.

Fasten off, leaving a long tail.

Embellishments:

With color B and a tapestry needle, embroider a face on the body.

With color C, embroider stitches to create the appearance of seams.

Assembly:

1. Stuff the body with fiberfill.

2. Sew the open end of the body closed.

Note: You can create variations by changing colors and adding different facial expressions.

This simple pattern instructs you to create a small amigurumi ball. The key is to follow each step, round by round, and piece by piece, to bring your amigurumi to life. As you gain experience, you'll be able to tackle more complex patterns and even design your own amigurumi creations.

Customizing Your Amigurumi

One of the most enjoyable aspects of amigurumi is the opportunity for personalization. Once you've mastered the basics, you can add your creative touch to your amigurumi projects. Here are some ways to customize your creations:

1. Color Choices

Experiment with different colors to create unique amigurumi. Color choice can significantly alter the character of your creation. Whether you're making a cute animal, a fantastical creature, or even a mini version of a loved one, colors play a vital role in character development.

2. Embellishments

You can add embellishments like bows, ribbons, tiny hats, or even miniature accessories to give your amigurumi a distinctive look. These little details can make your amigurumi stand out and add a touch of whimsy.

3. Facial Expressions

The embroidered or safety eyes, noses, and mouths give your amigurumi its personality. Experiment with different expressions to convey various emotions. A playful smile, curious eyes, or even a sly wink can all be used to create unique characters.

4. Accessories

Consider adding accessories like scarves, hats, or miniature props to your amigurumi. These elements can further define the story or theme of your creation.

Pattern Modifications

Once you've gained confidence in reading and following patterns, you can start modifying them to suit your vision. This can involve changing the size, shape, or style of your amigurumi to create something entirely your own. Remember that practice and experimentation are your allies in becoming a skilled amigurumi designer.

Creating Amigurumi for All Ages

Amigurumi is a versatile craft that can be enjoyed by crafters of all ages. Whether you're crafting for a child, a teenager, or an adult, there's a place for amigurumi in anyone's heart.

Amigurumi for Kids

Amigurumi toys make perfect companions for children. They're soft, huggable, and their small size makes them easy for little hands to hold. When creating amigurumi for kids, ensure all parts are securely attached, and avoid using small embellishments that could pose a choking hazard. Safety eyes and noses are often a better choice than sewn-on features.

Amigurumi for Teens

Teens enjoy amigurumi as both collectibles and décor. You can create trendy, character-inspired amigurumi that reflect their interests. Whether it's a favorite video game character or a cute anime figure, amigurumi can be a unique and personalized gift for teenagers.

Amigurumi for Adults

Adults often appreciate amigurumi as charming decorations, nostalgic keepsakes, or simply as an enjoyable and meditative craft. Consider creating amigurumi that evoke nostalgia or symbolize shared interests. For instance, an amigurumi of a beloved childhood cartoon character can make a thoughtful gift for an adult friend.

Starting Your First Project

Now that you're familiar with amigurumi patterns and customization options, it's time to dive into your first project. Here's a beginner-friendly amigurumi project that will help you practice the skills you've learned:

Amigurumi Heart Keychain

Materials:

Worsted weight yarn in any color

3.5mm crochet hook

Fiberfill stuffing

Keychain ring

Yarn needle

Instructions:

Heart (Make 2):

Round 1: With yarn, make a MR and SC 6 into the ring. (6)

Round 2: INC in each SC around. (12)

Round 3: (SC, INC) six times. (18)

Round 4: SC in each SC around. (18)

Assembly:

Stuff one heart lightly with fiberfill.

Place both hearts together, wrong sides facing, and slip stitch around the edges to join them.

Attach a keychain ring to the top.

This simple heart keychain makes a lovely gift or a cute accessory for your keys or bag. It's an excellent project for practicing the basic amigurumi techniques you've learned.

As you progress in your amigurumi journey, you'll have the opportunity to tackle more complex patterns and let your creativity shine. In the following chapters, we'll explore various amigurumi projects that span different skill levels, ensuring there's something for everyone on this delightful crafting adventure. Get ready to bring joy and warmth to the world, one amigurumi at a time.

Chapter 4: Eco-Conscious Amigurumi

In a world increasingly concerned about sustainability and environmental impact, amigurumi offers a unique opportunity to create with a conscience. Eco-conscious amigurumi is about crafting adorable characters while minimizing waste and choosing materials that are kinder to the planet. In this chapter, we'll explore the principles and practices of eco-conscious amigurumi and how you can contribute to a more sustainable world, one stitch at a time.

Selecting Eco-Friendly Yarn

The choice of yarn is a pivotal decision when creating eco-conscious amigurumi. Opting for environmentally friendly yarn options can make a significant difference in reducing your crafting footprint. Here are some considerations:

1. Organic Yarn

Organic yarn is produced without the use of synthetic pesticides and fertilizers. It's often made from cotton, bamboo, or hemp, and it's a sustainable choice for eco-conscious amigurumi. Look for certified organic yarn to ensure its authenticity.

2. Recycled Yarn

Recycled yarn is crafted from post-consumer or post-industrial textile waste, diverting materials from landfills. Some companies even specialize in upcycling old garments into beautiful new yarn. Using recycled yarn in your amigurumi not only conserves resources but also gives a second life to materials that would otherwise go to waste.

3. Sustainable Materials

Consider yarn made from sustainable fibers like bamboo, Tencel, and organic wool. These fibers are produced using environmentally friendly processes and renewable resources. By choosing sustainable materials, you contribute to reducing the environmental impact of your amigurumi projects.

Minimizing Waste

Eco-conscious amigurumi is about more than just yarn choice; it's also about reducing waste throughout your crafting process. Here are some strategies to minimize waste:

1. Plan Your Projects

Before you start, plan your amigurumi projects carefully. Consider the quantity of yarn you'll need and the colors required. By calculating your needs, you can avoid unnecessary yarn purchases and reduce leftover scraps.

2. Yarn Scraps

Collect and save small yarn scraps for future projects. Even the tiniest pieces can be useful for embroidering facial features, making tiny details, or creating multi-color amigurumi.

3. Repurpose Old Projects

If you have amigurumi projects that are no longer needed, consider unraveling them to reuse the yarn. It's an efficient way to reclaim yarn for future eco-conscious amigurumi endeavors.

4. Mindful Stitching

Pay attention to your stitching techniques to reduce the likelihood of errors and the need to unravel work, which can result in wasted yarn.

Eco-Friendly Stuffing

Fiberfill stuffing is a vital component of amigurumi, giving your creations their huggable, soft form. To make your amigurumi projects more eco-conscious, consider these alternatives to traditional synthetic fiberfill:

1. Recycled Fiberfill

Recycled fiberfill is crafted from post-consumer plastic bottles. It provides an eco-friendly option for stuffing your amigurumi, as it repurposes plastic waste while creating a soft and pliable filling.

2. Natural Fillings

You can also explore natural stuffing options, such as organic cotton or wool batting. These materials are biodegradable and free from synthetic chemicals. They offer a unique texture and are an ideal choice for those who prefer eco-conscious, all-natural amigurumi.

3. Fabric Scraps

Don't discard old fabric pieces. Small fabric scraps can be used as stuffing in your amigurumi projects. It's a great way to repurpose textiles and reduce waste.

Mindful Embellishments

When adding embellishments to your amigurumi, like safety eyes, noses, or other details, consider these eco-conscious practices:

1. Recycled Embellishments

Look for embellishments made from recycled or repurposed materials. Some manufacturers produce safety eyes and noses from recycled plastics, offering a sustainable choice for your amigurumi projects.

2. Handmade Embellishments

Consider crafting your embellishments using eco-friendly materials. For instance, you can make embroidered eyes or noses using organic embroidery thread or repurpose small buttons from old clothing.

Eco-Conscious Amigurumi Practices

In addition to selecting eco-friendly materials and reducing waste, there are broader practices that contribute to eco-conscious amigurumi:

1. Local Yarn Purchases

Support local yarn shops and artisans to reduce the carbon footprint associated with yarn transportation. Buying locally produced yarn also promotes regional economic sustainability.

2. Minimal Packaging

When purchasing yarn or materials, choose suppliers who use minimal or eco-friendly packaging. Many companies now offer products with reduced plastic and eco-conscious packaging materials.

3. Responsible Disposal

Consider the end of your amigurumi's life cycle. If a project is damaged beyond repair, try to recycle or upcycle the materials rather than disposing of them in landfills.

Sharing Eco-Conscious Amigurumi

Eco-conscious amigurumi isn't just a personal practice; it can be a way to inspire others to make sustainable choices in their crafting. Consider sharing your eco-conscious amigurumi journey through social media, blog posts, or community groups. By spreading awareness, you can encourage more crafters to adopt eco-friendly practices in their projects.

A Sustainable and Creative Journey

Eco-conscious amigurumi is a beautiful fusion of creativity and environmental responsibility. By making mindful choices in your materials, reducing waste, and adopting sustainable practices, you can create charming characters that not only bring joy to the world but also contribute to a healthier planet. As you continue on your amigurumi journey, remember that every stitch and every choice can make a difference in building a more sustainable crafting future.

Eco-Conscious Amigurumi Projects

To put eco-conscious principles into practice, let's explore a couple of amigurumi projects that align with sustainable crafting practices:

1. Upcycled Amigurumi

Why not transform old clothing or textiles into amigurumi characters? You can repurpose a beloved but worn-out sweater or T-shirt into a charming amigurumi friend. The process involves cutting the fabric into appropriate shapes and sewing them together, filling the amigurumi with eco-friendly stuffing. This project breathes new life into old textiles and reduces waste.

2. Plastic Bottle Amigurumi

Create amigurumi characters with a heartwarming message. Use plastic bottles as the core structure, stuffing them with recycled fiberfill or fabric scraps. The bottle serves as both the inner structure and a statement on repurposing plastic waste. Craft eco-conscious characters that reflect environmental themes, such as sea creatures or animals affected by pollution.

3. Eco-Friendly Critter Collection

Devote a series of amigurumi projects to eco-conscious critters. Craft animals like sea turtles, pandas, or endangered species and attach educational tags that share information about these creatures and their conservation needs. Promote environmental awareness through your amigurumi creations, and consider donating a portion of the proceeds to relevant conservation organizations.

Eco-Conscious Gift-Giving

Share the spirit of eco-conscious amigurumi by giving your creations as thoughtful, sustainable gifts. Craft amigurumi that align with the recipient's interests, values, or hobbies. For instance, if your friend loves marine life, create a set of amigurumi sea creatures from recycled materials.

Eco-Conscious Amigurumi Workshops

Consider organizing eco-conscious amigurumi workshops or classes within your local community or online. Teach others how to create eco-friendly amigurumi, share your knowledge about sustainable materials, and encourage participants to embrace these practices in their crafting journey. You can also host charity workshops to create amigurumi that are later donated to environmental causes.

Eco-conscious amigurumi represents an inspiring and responsible approach to crafting. It's about not only enjoying the art of amigurumi but also ensuring that our creative pursuits contribute positively to the world. As an eco-conscious amigurumi enthusiast, you have the power to make choices that reflect your commitment to sustainability and environmental stewardship. Your eco-friendly amigurumi can inspire others to join the movement, leading to a more sustainable and eco-aware crafting community. Together, we can create adorable characters while helping to preserve the planet for future generations.

Chapter 5: Patterns for Beginners

Embarking on your amigurumi journey as a beginner can be both exciting and rewarding. In this chapter, we'll explore a range of beginner-friendly amigurumi patterns designed to build your skills while creating adorable characters. Whether you're just starting or looking for simple projects to hone your craft, you'll find patterns that will guide you through the process step by step.

Amigurumi Essentials for Beginners

Before we dive into the patterns, let's review the essential materials and techniques that you'll need as a beginner:

Materials:

Worsted weight yarn in various colors

Appropriate crochet hook (typically 3.5mm to 4.0mm for worsted weight yarn)

Fiberfill stuffing

Opt for safety eyes or employ embroidery thread to craft the eyes and nose.s

Yarn needle

Scissors

Stitch markers (optional but helpful)

Techniques:

Magic Ring (MR) or Magic Circle

Single Crochet (SC)

Increase (INC) and Decrease (DEC)

Fastening Off

Sewing Amigurumi Parts

Weaving in Ends

With these basics in your toolkit, you're ready to begin crafting your first amigurumi character. Let's explore some beginner patterns to get you started.

Pattern 1: Amigurumi Ball

Materials:

Worsted weight yarn in your choice of color

3.5mm crochet hook

Fiberfill stuffing

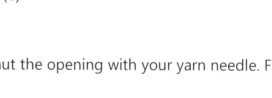

Instructions:

Round 1: Start with a magic ring, then crochet 6 single crochet (SC) stitches into the ring. (6)

Round 2: Increase (INC) in each SC around. (12)

Round 3: (SC, INC) six times. (18)

Round 4: (SC in each of the next 2 stitches, INC in the next stitch) six times. (24)

Rounds 5-8: SC in each stitch around. (24)

Round 9: (SC in each of the next 2 stitches, DEC) six times. (18)

Round 10: (SC, DEC) six times. (12)

Round 11: DEC in each stitch around. (6)

Fasten off and use the tail to seam shut the opening with your yarn needle. Fill the ball with fiberfill as you go.

This simple amigurumi ball is a great beginner project to help you practice shaping, increasing, and decreasing. You can experiment with different colors and yarn textures to create a variety of decorative balls.

Pattern 2: Amigurumi Cat

Materials:

Worsted weight yarn in desired cat color (body)

Worsted weight yarn in contrasting color (muzzle, paws, tail)

3.5mm crochet hook

Fiberfill stuffing

Safety eyes or embroidery thread for eyes and nose

Yarn needle

Scissors

Body:

Round 1: Start with a magic ring, crochet 6 SC into the ring. (6 stitches)

Round 2: INC in each SC around. (12 stitches)

Round 3: SC, INC repeat 6 times. (18 stitches)

Round 4: SC in each stitch around. (18 stitches)

Round 5: SC in next 2 stitches, INC repeat 6 times. (24 stitches)

Rounds 6-10: SC in each stitch around. (24 stitches per round)

Round 11: SC in next 2 stitches, DEC repeat 6 times. (18 stitches)

Round 12: SC, DEC repeat 6 times. (12 stitches)

Finish off, leaving a long tail for sewing. Stuff the body firmly with fiberfill before closing the opening.

Muzzle:

Round 1: Start with a magic ring, crochet 6 SC into the ring. (6 stitches)

Finish off, leaving a long tail for sewing. Attach the muzzle to the lower part of the face, positioning it between where the eyes will be. Embroider or attach the eyes and nose above the muzzle.

Paws (Make 4):

Round 1: Start with a magic ring, crochet 5 SC into the ring. (5 stitches)

Finish off, leaving a tail for sewing. Sew the paws to the body, two on each side.

Tail:

Row 1: Chain 5, SL ST in the 2nd chain from the hook and in the remaining chains.

Finish off, leaving a tail for sewing. Attach the tail to the back of the body.

Assembly and Finishing:

After attaching all parts, use the yarn needle to weave in any loose ends.

For a more expressive face, consider adding whiskers or shaping the face with some gentle stitches through the head.

Pattern 3: Amigurumi Flower

Materials:

Worsted weight yarn in your choice of colors (flower,

3.5mm crochet hook

Fiberfill stuffing (optional, for the stem)

Yarn needle

Scissors

Flower Center:

Round 1: Start with a magic ring, crochet 5 SC into the ring. (5 stitches)

Round 2: INC in each SC around. (10 stitches)

Round 3: SC, INC repeat 5 times. (15 stitches)

Round 4: SC in next 2 stitches, INC repeat 5 times. (20 stitches)

Round 5: SC in next 3 stitches, INC repeat 5 times. (25 stitches)

Rounds 6-8: SC in each stitch around. (25 stitches per round)

Finish off, leaving a long tail for sewing if needed.

Petals (Make 5 or more):

Row 1: Chain 6, turn.

Row 2: Starting from the second chain from the hook, SL ST in the first chain, SC in the next, HDC (half double crochet) in the next, DC (double crochet) in the next, and finish with a TR (treble crochet) in the last chain. Chain 1, turn.

Work back down the other side of the chain, mirroring the stitches: TR, DC, HDC, SC, and SL ST.

Finish off, leaving a tail for sewing.

Attach the petals around the edge of the flower center.

Stem (Optional):

Row 1: Chain to your desired stem length.

Row 2: SC in the second chain from the hook and in each chain across.

Finish off, optionally stuff lightly with fiberfill, and attach to the back of the flower.

Assembly and Finishing:

Sew the petals around the flower center, spacing them evenly.

If you made a stem, attach it to the back of the flower.

Weave in any loose ends with your yarn needle.

This pattern creates a simple and cute amigurumi flower, perfect for beginners. You can play with different colors for the petals and center to create a variety of flowers. Enjoy your crocheting!

Pattern 4: Amigurumi Teddy Bear
Materials:

- Worsted weight yarn in bear color (body, head)
- Worsted weight yarn in a contrasting color (muzzle, paws, ears)
- 3.5mm crochet hook
- Fiberfill stuffing
- Safety eyes or embroidery thread for eyes and nose
- Yarn needle
- Scissors

Body:

1. **Round 1:** Start with a magic ring, crochet 6 SC into the ring. (6 stitches)
2. **Round 2:** INC in each SC around. (12 stitches)
3. **Round 3:** *SC, INC* repeat 6 times. (18 stitches)
4. **Round 4:** *SC in next 2 stitches, INC* repeat 6 times. (24 stitches)
5. **Rounds 5-11:** SC in each stitch around. (24 stitches per round)
6. **Round 12:** *SC in next 2 stitches, DEC* repeat 6 times. (18 stitches)

Finish off, leaving a long tail for sewing. Stuff the body with fiberfill and seam shut the opening.

Head:

Follow the same pattern as the body for Rounds 1-12. Then:

7.   **Rounds 13-19:** SC in each stitch around. (18 stitches per round)
8.   **Round 20:** *SC, DEC* repeat 6 times. (12 stitches)
Stuff the head firmly with fiberfill before closing. Attach safety eyes or embroider eyes and nose before finishing off.

Muzzle:

1.   **Round 1:** Start with a magic ring, crochet 6 SC into the ring. (6 stitches)
Finish off, leaving a tail for sewing. Attach the muzzle to the head, below the eyes.

Paws (Make 4):

1.   **Round 1:** Start with a magic ring, crochet 5 SC into the ring. (5 stitches)
Finish off, leaving a tail for sewing. Attach the paws to the body.

Ears (Make 2):

1.   **Round 1:** Start with a magic ring, crochet 6 SC into the ring. (6 stitches)
Finish off, leaving a tail for sewing. Attach the ears to the top of the head.

Assembly and Finishing:

- Sew the head to the body.
- Attach the muzzle, ears, and paws to their respective positions.
- Use the yarn needle to weave in all loose ends.

Pattern 5: Amigurumi Heart

Materials:

Worsted weight yarn in your choice of color

3.5mm crochet hook

Fiberfill stuffing

Yarn needle

Scissors

Instructions:

First, make two lobes for the top of the heart. Each lobe is made separately, then joined together.

Lobe (Make 2):

Round 1: Start with a magic ring, crochet 6 SC into the ring. (6 stitches)

Round 2: INC in each SC around. (12 stitches)

Round 3: SC, INC repeat 6 times. (18 stitches)

Round 4: SC in each stitch around. (18 stitches)

Do not finish off the second lobe. Instead, continue to join the lobes:

Joining Lobes:

Chain 1, then SC in each stitch around the first lobe. Continue to SC in each stitch of the second lobe. (36 stitches)

Body of Heart:

Round 5: SC in each of the next 4 stitches, INC repeat 7 times, SC in the last 2 stitches. (42 stitches)

Round 6: SC in each stitch around. (42 stitches)

Round 7: SC in each of the next 5 stitches, DEC repeat 6 times. (36 stitches)

Round 8: SC in each of the next 4 stitches, DEC repeat 6 times. (30 stitches)

Round 9: SC in each of the next 3 stitches, DEC repeat 6 times. (24 stitches)

Round 10: SC in each of the next 2 stitches, DEC repeat 6 times. (18 stitches)

Round 11: SC, DEC repeat 6 times. (12 stitches)

Stuff the heart firmly with fiberfill.

Finishing:

Round 12: DEC six times. (6 stitches)

Finish off, leaving a long tail. Use the yarn needle to close the remaining opening and to shape the bottom point of the heart.

Pattern 6: Amigurumi Octopus
Materials:

Worsted weight yarn in your choice of colors

3.5mm crochet hook

Fiberfill stuffing

Safety eyes or embroidery thread for eyes

Yarn needle

Scissors

Head:

Round 1: Start with a magic ring, crochet 6 SC into the ring. (6 stitches)

Round 2: INC in each SC around. (12 stitches)

Round 3: SC, INC repeat 6 times. (18 stitches)

Round 4: SC in next 2 stitches, INC repeat 6 times. (24 stitches)

Rounds 5-8: SC in each stitch around. (24 stitches per round)

Finish off, leaving a long tail for sewing. Stuff the shut the opening.

Legs (Make 8):

Round 1: Start with a magic ring, crochet 6 SC into

Rounds 2-6: SC in each stitch around. (6 stitches pe

Round 7: SC in the next 2 stitches, 3 SC in the r stitches)

Rounds 8-15: SC in each stitch around. (10 stitches per round)

Finish off, leaving a tail for sewing. To give the legs a curled appearance, fold them and use a few stitches at the end of each leg to hold the fold in place.

Assembly and Finishing:

Attach safety eyes or embroider the eyes on the head.

Sew the legs evenly around the bottom of the head. Ensure the folded part of the legs faces downwards to mimic the curl of octopus legs.

Use the yarn needle to weave in any loose ends.

Pattern 7: Amigurumi Mushroom

Materials:

Worsted weight yarn in mushroom cap color

Worsted weight yarn in a contrasting color for the stem

3.5mm crochet hook

Fiberfill stuffing

Yarn needle

Scissors

Cap:

Round 1: Start with a magic ring, crochet 6 SC into the ring. (6 stitches)

Round 2: INC in each SC around. (12 stitches)

Round 3: SC, INC repeat 6 times. (18 stitches)

Round 4: SC in next 2 stitches, INC repeat 6 times. (24 stitches)

Rounds 5-6: SC in each stitch around. (24 stitches per round)

Finish off, leaving a long tail for sewing. Stuff the cap lightly with fiberfill and seam shut the opening.

Stem:

Round 1: Start with a magic ring, crochet 6 SC into the ring. (6 stitches)

Rounds 2-3: SC in each stitch around. (6 stitches per round)

Round 4: SC in next 2 stitches, INC repeat twice. (8 stitches)

Rounds 5-10: SC in each stitch around. (8 stitches per round)

Finish off, leaving a long tail for sewing. Stuff the stem with a small amount of fiberfill for stability.

Assembly and Finishing:

Sew the stem to the center of the underside of the cap. Ensure the seam is neat and secure.

Optionally, you can embroider small white dots on the cap to mimic the appearance of some mushroom species.

Use the yarn needle to weave in any loose ends.

Pattern 8: Amigurumi Star

Materials:

Worsted weight yarn in your choice of color

3.5mm crochet hook

Fiberfill stuffing

Yarn needle

Scissors

Instructions:

Star Center:

Round 1: Start with a magic ring, crochet 5 SC into the ring. (5 stitches)

Round 2: INC in each SC around. (10 stitches)

Round 3: SC, INC repeat 5 times. (15 stitches)

Round 4: SC in next 2 stitches, INC repeat 5 times. (20 stitches)

Round 5: SC in each stitch around. (20 stitches)

Do not finish off. Proceed to create the points of the star.

Star Points (Make 5):

Each point is made directly from the star center.

Row 1: Chain 1, then make 3 SC in the next 3 stitches. Turn.

Row 2: Chain 1, DEC, SC in the last stitch. Turn.

Row 3: Chain 1, DEC. Turn.

Row 4: Chain 1, then make 1 SC.

Finish off the point and sew the small hole at the base of the point closed. Reattach yarn in the next stitch of the star center and repeat for the remaining 4 points.

Finishing:

After completing all five points, stuff each point lightly with fiberfill before closing.

Ensure that the star center is flat; do not stuff the center.

Use the yarn needle to weave in any loose ends and to shape the star as necessary.

Pattern 9: Amigurumi Ice Cream Cone
Materials:

Worsted weight yarn in cone color and ice cream scoop colors

3.5mm crochet hook

Fiberfill stuffing

Yarn needle

Scissors

Cone:

Round 1: Start with a magic ring, crochet 6 SC into the ring. (6 stitches)

Round 2: INC in each SC around. (12 stitches)

Rounds 3-5: SC in each stitch around. (12 stitches per round)

Round 6: SC in the next stitch, INC repeat 6 times. (18 stitches)

Rounds 7-12: SC in each stitch around. (18 stitches per round)

Finish off, leaving a long tail for sewing. The cone should have a tapered shape.

Scoop (Make 2 or more):

Round 1: Start with a magic ring, crochet 6 SC into the ring. (6 stitches)

Round 2: INC in each SC around. (12 stitches)

Round 3: SC, INC repeat 6 times. (18 stitches)

Round 4: SC in each stitch around. (18 stitches)

Round 5: SC in next 2 stitches, DEC repeat 6 times. (12 stitches)

Stuff each scoop lightly with fiberfill.

Finish off, leaving a long tail for sewing.

Assembly:

Sew the first scoop on top of the cone, making sure it's centered.

Sew the second scoop on top of the first, aligning it so that the ice cream looks stacked.

Optionally, embroider some details on the cone to mimic the waffle pattern.

Pattern 10: Amigurumi Apple

Materials:

Worsted weight yarn in apple color (body)

Worsted weight yarn in green color (leaf)

Worsted weight yarn in brown color (stem)

3.5mm crochet hook

Fiberfill stuffing

Yarn needle

Scissors

Body:

Round 1: Start with a magic ring, crochet 6 SC

Round 2: INC in each SC around. (12 stitches)

Round 3: SC, INC repeat 6 times. (18 stitches)

Round 4: SC in next 2 stitches, INC repeat 6 tir

Rounds 5-10: SC in each stitch around. (24 stitches per round)

Finish off, leaving a long tail for sewing. Stuff the apple with fiberfill and seam shut the opening.

Leaf:

Round 1: Start with a magic ring, crochet 6 SC into the ring. (6 stitches)

Round 2: SC, INC repeat 3 times. (9 stitches)

Rounds 3-4: SC in each stitch around. (9 stitches)

Finish off, leaving a tail for sewing. Attach the leaf to the top of the apple.

Stem:

Row 1: Chain 6.

Row 2: SC in the second chain from the hook and in each chain across. (5 SC)

Finish off, leaving a tail for sewing. Attach the stem to the top of the apple, near the leaf.

Assembly and Finishing:

Sew the leaf and stem onto the top of the apple, securing them firmly.

Use the yarn needle to weave in any loose ends.

In the following sections of this chapter, we'll explore more beginner patterns that introduce additional techniques and concepts, allowing you to progress in your amigurumi crafting skills.

SCAN THIS QR CODE TO DOWLOAD 40+ AMIGURUMI PATTERNS, THE GRANNY SQUARE EBOOK AND THE FULL COLORED VERSION OF THIS BOOK

Scan me

Chapter 6: Final Thoughts and Next Steps

As we come to the end of this journey into the world of amigurumi, it's time to reflect on what we've learned, created, and celebrated. This chapter serves as a space for final thoughts, encouragement, and guidance for your future amigurumi endeavors. We'll explore the many ways you can continue to expand your skills, grow your amigurumi collection, and share your love for this art form with others.

Reflecting on Your Amigurumi Journey

Whether you're a seasoned amigurumi artist or just starting, it's important to take a moment to reflect on your creative journey. What have you discovered about yourself, your crafting style, and the joy of bringing amigurumi to life? Think about the patterns you've completed, the challenges you've overcome, and the unique touches you've added to your creations. Your amigurumi collection is a testament to your growth as a maker.

Finding Inspiration in Nature

Nature is a boundless source of inspiration for amigurumi. From animals and plants to the elements, you can draw from the beauty of the natural world to create unique and captivating amigurumi. Consider crafting animals like foxes, owls, or bears, or bring the charm of flowers and succulents into your amigurumi garden. The colors, textures, and shapes found in nature are an endless well of creative ideas.

Diving into Fantasy and Fiction

Amigurumi offers the perfect canvas for bringing your favorite fictional characters and fantastical creatures to life. Whether you're a fan of classic literature, movies, or video games, you can explore the world of pop culture through amigurumi. Craft beloved characters like Harry Potter, Pikachu, or your favorite superheroes. Embrace the magic of fantasy and let your imagination soar.

Spreading Joy with Amigurumi Gifts

One of the most beautiful aspects of amigurumi is the ability to create personalized gifts for your loved ones. Consider gifting amigurumi creations for birthdays, anniversaries, and special occasions. A handcrafted amigurumi gift is not only a symbol of your love and care but also a unique and cherished keepsake. The smile on the recipient's face is the most rewarding part of the process.

Sharing the Art of Amigurumi

Passing on your amigurumi knowledge is a wonderful way to give back to the crafting community. Consider hosting amigurumi workshops or creating tutorials to guide others on their own amigurumi adventures. Sharing patterns and techniques not only enriches the community but also ensures that the art of amigurumi continues to flourish.

Exploring Advanced Techniques

Once you've mastered the basics, don't hesitate to dive into more advanced amigurumi techniques. Experiment with intricate stitches, gradient yarn, and color changes to elevate your creations. Explore amigurumi garments, accessories, and oversized amigurumi for a new level of challenge and creativity.

Setting Amigurumi Goals

Setting goals for your amigurumi projects can be motivating and rewarding. Whether it's completing a certain number of patterns in a year, crafting a specific collection, or learning a challenging technique, having goals can push you to expand your skills and enjoy the sense of accomplishment that comes with each achievement.

Amigurumi for Charity

Consider using your amigurumi talents to make a difference in the lives of others. Many crafters create amigurumi to donate to charities and organizations that support children, the elderly, or those in need. Your creations can bring comfort and joy to those facing difficult circumstances.

Made in United States
Orlando, FL
30 December 2024

56627798R00072